THE RAD
OF
JAHNETS

JAHNETS

EXPRESSO
331 Newman Springs Road,
Red Bank, New Jersey, 07701
1-888-251-6088 ext 101
info@expressopublishing.com

In loving appreciation
to all those who have
supported me in all ways
both throughout my Rad
and with this publication.

Osiris
Jupiter
Prometheus
Rama
JWP
Aleister Crowley
Sonja Elliott
Elta
Alex
Amber
Connie
My mother

and others too many to mention

Introduction

This novel is a partial autobiography of the magical side of my life, and what I have learned from it. I hope that in the telling of it some superstitions are laid to rest that I have noticed forming in public views recently like those of aliens wanting to take over the Earth. If you could change into any shape you wished, would that change what you are inside?

All of the experiences I have written in this book happened to me, as I say, with only the names changed to protect those who are fearful of what exposure could do to their present life style. I am writing this for those people who are having, or have had similar experiences, so they know they are not alone, they are not crazy, over imaginative, or any of the other names people call you when they are afraid. Although a few dear friends, and family members did tell me as far back as high school that I should write a book about my experiences, I have always felt like the majority of people do not believe me anyway so what would be the point? To expose myself to ridicule and not have anyone gain anything from it seemed a waste. It has only been in the last few years that I realized it did not matter anymore, that there will always be those who are simply not ready and can not open themselves up to change. I know now that if you are meant to get this you will, and if you are not meant to get it, then nothing anyone says or does will change your mind. I have shown what I was allowed to show to people, only to have them a few weeks later get talked out of what they saw by their own or someone else's ego. This to me is utterly amazing. Until you experience a friend, loved one or family being with you while something of this nature occurs and then later saying something like, "I am not really sure anymore, I mean I saw it, but how can that be? There must be a logical reason for this, no one will believe you anyway," you just have no comprehension of the hurt it causes. Maybe it was a test of courage and honor for them that they failed, who knows. All I know is that what some humans have done to millions of people because they saw a UFO, a Faerie, a Gray, a Reptile, or any other type of being different from the norm was a great wrong and will incur them like Karma. So with that in mind, they may want to pass this book on to someone who they think could use it after they have read it of course. That way even if it is another lifetime that the Karma hits them, the information will make its way back to you when you need it. Intention means everything...

For the record, I would not have traded this life for any other because I have learned so much and had such great friends. Even though I have had do deal with ridicule and harassment from some humans, I have evolved so much from my friendships with other beings that I have never felt truly alone.

People often ask why the aliens do not just show up, and I have answered this to the best of my abilities. Hopefully enough souls will wake up to the fact that we are the children of two groups, and probably the cousins of others so that we can live and learn from one another. It is my dearest wish that the magic will come back to Earth now. I believe that this is the next step for humanity in their evolution. Humans need to realize how they are creating their world with their thoughts and feelings. When they do, the natural evolution of that will be the true magical experiences like those of Merlin. First humanity has to take back control of their world from the ego. The brain is a tool meant to help the soul with the body while it is still developing, so that it lives to adulthood. Not to run your life and make your decisions. Imagination is more than just a fanciful children's pastime. It is a tool the soul uses to create it's world with the help of the spirit. Each human is a body with a soul and a spirit and as such we are all one. We all may need to learn different lessons in different ways, and this is ok. The brain was meant to be a translator and receiver for the communications between the spirit(mind) and the soul(heart) and to keep those experiences in memory. You, the real you, is the *soul,* and the soul and spirit will merge one day when you both have found a way to see each other as equal. When that happens you will become enlightened. You will become a different being. The body is like the shell of an egg with a sperm and ova in it. One day the shell breaks and a new being emerges. You need your body until you merge with your spirit like a chicken needs the egg shell until it grows into a chick. The ego being the translator, receiver with a memory does not understand that it will merge with the rest into a new form, because it is not in it's memory. It sees itself as part of the body, and that is it's primary focus. The ego has learned that the soul creates using the imagination, and so takes control of the souls imagination by getting the soul to focus on what it thinks is of value. But the ego(brain) thinks it is part of the body. You are not the body, you are what animates the body, and your values are different. Yet you are allowing your ego to decide your life for you by allowing it to direct your focus. How can the spirit admire the soul and see it as equal when the soul allows the ego to steal it's imagination and create that which it does not want? Have compassion for those egos who do not get this, they truly know not what they do.

In closing let me say it is my greatest wish that this novel will help many people to understand better what they are, and by doing so make the effort to take back their imagination and change their life for the better. Barring that I hope you at least enjoy it.

Chapter One

The first time I can remember being spoken to telepathically, I was three. My family and I were going to the beach and I was trailing behind. The sand was hot on my feet and it was the first time I had ever seen the ocean. It was the Atlantic Ocean, and we were at Long Beach, New York. My mother and sister kept saying come on Jahnets keep up with us, but the ocean seemed alive to me and I could not help stopping to stare at it. I felt like it was going to reach right out and grab me and I could not understand what was holding it back. While I stared, my family walked to a spot to sit the blankets and chairs down. This beach is a really big beach and there were thousands of people there that day. I turned to look for them and they were out of site. I was frantically scanning the crowd and could not see one of them. That was when I heard the voice. There was a young woman and her boyfriend lying on towels in front of me and she was watching me. She seemed nice but they were strangers. I heard a voice say,

"Go on you can trust her, she will help you to a safe place." I looked around trying to figure out who was talking to me and could not. She did help, and I sat in the lost kids corral all day waiting. This was just the beginning...

My father was in the Air Force and by the time I was five, he was stationed at George Air Force Base. We lived on the outskirts of Victorville, California on the Mohave Desert. One day my father brought home, a tent and canteen from his work and set it up for me. My mother would not let me go in it though because scorpions and tarantulas crawled into shady places to escape the sun. Instead, I began pretending to be lost in the desert with only a canteen. Being tomboyish, I would catch horny toads and lizards and would try to catch the jackrabbits but they were too fast. I walked across the road and out of site of the house so I could imagine properly that I was lost, after all you can not pretend to be lost and be able to see your home. Maybe these were not really my thoughts but theirs, but these are the thoughts that came to me and that I believed at the time to be mine. Then the water became hot in the canteen and I thought this was no fun. I was looking at the ground like I always did for Horny

Toads to catch and next thing I know I am waking up on a metal table. There are four to five short doctors in white lab coats on my left and two nurses on my right. The doctors kept flashing in and out so that one moment they would be doctors and the next blue dwarf guys in lab coats with dark hair. While they were humanoid, looking their faces looked more like a dwarfs and their skin was a medium blue and they had black hair that did not look combed well. I sat there staring at them, and when they came closer, I would scream "NO" every time they got to a certain point. When I screamed, they were driven back by the force of my voice through swinging doors like a wind would do. That this had worked gave me courage that I could protect myself somewhat and was not completely out numbered. This happened maybe four times and one of the nurses on my right said, "You know you cannot keep doing that." He/ she spoke telepathically to me and when I looked at her one minute she would be a blonde-haired woman and the next a gray alien. I was quite a handful as a kid and did not like being told I was not capable of anything and I screamed at him, "Oh yes I can, you just watch", and I screamed at the little blue guys again and knocked them back through the doors. (What he had done and I want to point out here is plant a thought in my mind, and though I realized he was doing something even as a child I did not quite understand at that time how he did it). I realized he was right though, my voice would tire, and irritated that he was going to win I said, "What do they want?" The nurse/gray told me, "We need to put something in your throat so we will be able to find you." Along with this thought was another thought that they would not be able to find me and I would get lost and that they wanted to watch over me.

All this time the little blue beings were standing down by the doors waiting for my answer. I answered him with, "Well ok but they don't have to be so mean about it." Every time I knocked them back, they would get this look of someone pushing against great odds or wind and of course, their faces would look strained and scary to me. Toe gray looked toward the blues and they started smiling a kind of goofy smile and slowly walked up to me. They reached me and gently pushed me down on the table so I would be still and I opened my mouth and I choked as they stuck something up in my adenoid area. That made me mad again because I figured that they should be able to do it without choking me, and the gray said," It's ok, you won't remember any of this tomorrow." I was angry at this point and said, "Oh yes I will, I will remember this if it's the last thing I ever do." I could almost see his eyes smiling behind the blackness.

The next thing I was lying in the sand and it was so warm I did not want to wake up. A voice kept telling me to get up, but I was so comfortable I did not want to move. More urgently, the voice said, "If you don't get up the snakes and scorpions will get you." At this, I opened my eyes and was afraid of moving at first because snakes and scorpions will attack if you move or so I had been taught. I remember asking if there was one, but I don't remember if ljust thought it in my mind and he answered or if l said it out loud but he answered, ''No, but if you lay there much longer they will find you." So I jumped up quick, looked around, and noticed I was further than I remembered being from home, I grabbed the canteen that was lying in the sand next to me and began walking. The water in the canteen was hot by this time and I could not even drink it.

I made it home, my mother was upset asking me where I had been, and telling me, that everyone had been out looking for me. I told her I was across the road and way out almost to the dump and she was even more upset I was so far out.

It was weeks after this, that my mother was sewing in the living room and my father was reading the paper. I was sitting on the floor at his feet and for some reason staring at the light.

You know how you will look at something, a memory is on the tip of your mind, and you keep staring at the object trying to see it or remember what it is? Well I was staring at this light for the same reason. The memories were tugging at my mind. I must have hypnotized myself as I fell asleep there and woke screaming at the top of my lungs and fighting my father who was trying to stop me from kicking over the lamp by getting hold of me. I was fighting blues trying to hold me down... I told him all about it and he seemed to believed me. My mother did not. My father believed me so much we took a ride to where I told him it happened in our car, and there was a high school there. I told them it was not at the school, and then became confused because I knew I was in a room that looked like a hospital room in this general direction and there were not many buildings in that direction then. Victorville was just beginning to grow but was still a Podunk little town. My mother convinced them all it was a nightmare, but my father looked at me and I could tell he knew something he was not telling and he looked angry.

After this happened, I remember being frightened to sleep in my room for a while. My younger sister and I had bunk beds, and I was on top and could see things coming up to the window at night. I remember saying a little man was out there. Then my younger sister saw one. Mother thought she was just copying me and we had probably seen jack rabbits, so I was chastised further for being a bad example and scaring my little sister. Some days later our garden of carrots under my window came up eaten by jack rabbits making my mothers explanation appear correct. My mother never did see them and so never believed me. I tried going under the covers but I could hear them saying, "You can't hide under the covers, how are they going to protect you." I would finally pass out after lying there for a while. There was nothing else I could do but accept it for the time being, until I could figure out how to prove it to the rest of my family.

During first grade I took a bus to school, and I had to walk up a block to catch it at a comer. The girl who lived at the comer was much older than I, and my mother would not let me play with her for that reason. She felt she would teach me things older kids were doing. She and I were waiting at the bus stop when the son of my mothers' best friend decided to come down the street to our stop. An argwnent started when the older girl told him to go back to his stop. He started throwing rocks. Then we were all throwing rocks. A number of times during the rock fight I heard a voice telling me to stop, and would look around but never see anyone. It was a male's voice. In the end, the boy threw a big rock and hit me in the leg. The older girl grabbed it, threw it, and missed. I looked around but there was no more ammunition and all I could find to throw was a surveyor's broken stick. By this time, he knew I was mad because he had hit me, and was running down the road. I really did not think I could hit him but was so angry I was going to try rather than let him get away with it. I figured at least it would land close and scare him. I threw

the stick up in the air in his direction, gauging the angle as

you would a pool shot. How I knew to do this in first grade,

I do not know, I just did. The older girl and I watched as the

stick went way up in the air and then came down and he fell.

We both looked at each other with our mouths open, and she

said," Did you just hit him with that stick?" It was so far we

could not believe it and we could not see for sure. Then he

picked himself up off the ground and went running towards

his bus stop, and we both thought he had just tripped. About

that time, the bus came over the rise in the road and picked

us up and continued up the road. Then the driver saw the boy

at his stop with blood all over. We both were escorted to the

principals' office and told we were going to jail. They called

the police and one officer and then the other one interrogated

me. For a six or seven year old, this was quite traumatic not to

mention it was my mothers best friends son. The only saving

grace was that no one could believe I threw it that far, even

though I had told them I had. My mothers friend forgave me

and did not press charges, which was nice considering her son,

had to be operated on to get the stick out of his head. I learned the hard way that when I did not listen to the voice I got in trouble. I thought the voice was God or my guardian angel and so tried to listen after that. I also thought everyone heard this as I had been told everyone had a guardian angel. I think this is important to point out because there are too many out there, who seem to think the grays' were cold and callas and my gray never was. I believe that when I became lucid on the table and later remembered it they saw and so kept a closer watch on me.

My father and I got on great because we were alike in many ways. He was a Leo and so was I, with our birthdays just days apart. He was also very intuitive. One day he came home early from work and was sitting at the kitchen table. He was about to go into the back yard and survey the area for the best place for a badminton court, and I wanted to go with him, but my mother said no, that he needed to spend more time with my little sister. He could see the disappointment on my face. Mother was always working around the house, cleaning or cooking or sewing and never had time for me, or so I felt. My father agreed and walked out the back door with my sister and my mother would not even let me look from the window. I felt betrayed. We were suppose to move to Anchorage pretty soon and they had already taken my dog to the pound. They said it was because we were moving, but my little sister had tried to take a bone away from the dog twice and the dog snapped at her. My mother never liked animals much and due to my little sister I felt I was loosing everything. Maybe my mother felt I wanted all the attention due to the differences between her Scorpio personality and my Leo personality, or maybe she saw her mother in me since my grandmother was a Leo too. She always seemed more critical of me, and thought I was too hyper. I finally made some excuse and got out the back door, but she followed me saying to stay away from my father and sister. So I watched from behind an icicle plant bank getting angrier and angrier by the minute. I could not understand why we could not all be together at once. I felt my mother was mean and did not approve of me and my father had listened to her and betrayed me. As I was standing there glaring at them from behind a hill, I remember thinking I wish he would trip and fall. Then I saw him stumble and fall. I immediately felt remorse and that I had caused it. I went running into the house yelling, "Mother, Daddy fell." My mother dropped the kitchen towel and followed me out the back door. About that time they were coming up towards the house. He said he had tripped over a bramble bush and hit his head. He looked over at me for tattling on him and said he was fine.

A few weeks later my father collapsed at home and they rushed him to the hospital. He had an aneurysm burst in the front of his head. We were about to move to Anchorage and this was the only thing that saved us from being in that really bad earthquake they had up there in the sixties. Before you think God works in mysterious ways, I will say I do not think loosing my father and my dog, was a fair trade. They took him to the big naval hospital at San Diego to operate on him and we were told it was a miracle he made it. We drove to San Diego to see him once and my mother took us to the San Diego Zoo while we were there.

Chapter Two

Life went on while he was gone, though my mother was always busy cleaning or doing something. So I played in the yard or on the hill behind our house looking for horny toads and lizards. There was a deep crevasse behind our hill and between another rise and looked like something I could pretend I was a mountain climber on. It had holes all along the side walls and I was more than half way up it and suddenly had the thought that a tarantula could be in one of those holes, and froze there in fear. I thought about jumping down but it was a long way, too far I thought and I was only a couple of feet from the top, but would have to stick my hand in another hole to get to the top . As I was gauging my options, a man appeared standing at the top about ten feet from me across the cleft and looking down at me. This was no ordinary man and even I could see that as young as I was. He had long dark hair before long hair was popular and was beautiful and was dressed fancy like King Louis. He spoke to me, asking me what I was doing and saying something about the holes and it was dangerous as there might be tarantulas in them and that I should jump down. While he spoke to me, he was looking around as though he was making sure no one else was about to overhear us. I was at a point where I could not go anywhere without sticking my hand in the hole, since it was too far down to jump without risking getting hurt. I remember looking at him and saying, "Why don't you just give me a hand up?" Him saying, "I don't think I will do that." I asked him, "why?" He said something about I had gotten myself into this situation and would have to get myself out. That made me angry because it made me feel like he did not care anyway, and I steeled my nerve and quickly stuck my hand in the hole and jumped up to face him and he was gone. I looked all over for him and he was gone, and it seemed impossible to me. He could not have gotten that far in the middle of the desert, and I was standing on top of the hill and could see. Of course, I made the mistake of telling my mother, and she of course told me I could not go there any more. She thought he was a bum or something, or I would fall and no one would know where I was. I knew he was not.

Bums are not beautiful they look dirty and like they slept in their clothes and he did not look dirty, he looked like royalty with a white lace shirt with lacey cuffs and a darker cape. I thought about him a lot, wondering where he came from and where he went. I finally decided he was my guardian angel.

Any help I was getting from them was in giving me encouragement or challenging me to do for myself I did not know who he was for certain but since then I have asked others and was told he was a guard set to watch an entry way. Maybe the hill was more than just a hill. When I think back on all of the things that happened to me where I actually saw these beings and spoke to them, not in trance or a vision but with them appearing out of nowhere, I had to wonder why me, how did they know me? For most of the rest of my life I would be asking myself this question. It would push me in this occult direction in order to find out, for no one else wanted to talk about it or investigate it. It was because they were afraid I knew, but they had not seen them or talked to them. I had never felt threaten by them at all and I just could not understand this attitude.

When my father finally came home from the hospital it had been months and he wanted to surprise my mother so he took a taxi. We were living on the outskirts of the town down the road from the closest neighbor, so a woman with her three daughters is going to be a little skittish especially at night. It was nighttime, and there comes a knock at the door. I yelled to my mother that someone was at the door and she yelled back from the back of the house, "Ask who it is." I did, but there was no answer. Suddenly I could hear my father saying, "Lucy", and rushed to open the door, saying, "It's Daddy, it's Daddy". My older sister who as I recall was at the kitchen table doing homework and my mother came running and yelling at the same time saying I did not know who it was and I better not open that door. They were furious with me and scared. I told them it was daddy and they said, "How do you know, did you hear him?" and I said, "Yes I heard him". Well no one else had heard anything so neither of them believed me. Then my mother goes to the door and says, "Who's there?" and my father answers her. She turned around, wide eyed and says, "How did you know? He said something didn't he? How did you know?" As if someone was playing a bad joke on her. In the mean time my father is saying, "Is someone going to let me in?" Once in, he looks at me strangely as my mother is trying to relate what just happened. He says, "I never said anything because I wanted to surprise you." At this point, I am in tears for being yelled at and no one believing me when I really had heard him. This too was just the beginning. My father hushed me and asked me what I heard. I told him I could hear him saying, "Lucy", which was my mothers' middle name that he always called her by to tease her. He said he had been standing there practicing what he was going to say internally when my mom came to the door, but he had not said anything aloud because he wanted to surprise her. My mothers over reaction towards me in fear had made me feel like I had done something wrong. I am not sure why, but my mother was always afraid of her own intuition though she knew she had it also. Almost like she thought it was a curse and by her thinking something it would happen. She never voiced this except for indirectly when she had dreams about us through the years she would call and say she just had a nightmare about us.

When we asked what she dreamed about, she would not tell us, like talking about it would make it come true. Although my father was home, he was not the same. He had a horse shoe scar on his head where they had operated on him and he limped a little. He also had to take medicine so that the vein would not leak and cause him to have more seizures. He retired from the Air Force shortly after that and we moved to Richmond, California in the Bay Area where his parents lived so family would be close by. He became epileptic due to all this and occasionally would have a seizure if he forgot his medicine. He could not drive, because back then they took your license in case you had a seizure while you were driving. He also had a hard time finding a job because of the liability to companies insurance. We stayed at his parents for a while until my parents found a house to rent a few blocks away. My grandparents house had deer and moose heads in the living room, and grand father and grand mother clocks that chimed every quarter of an hour, and I hated sleeping in the same room with the heads staring at me. It was not until I was much older that I realized the reason I felt like the deer heads were staring at me was because of the shape of the eyes. We rented a house a few blocks away from his parents and lived there for a few years.

I was always playing in the street out front our house with the other kids around the block. We played kick ball a lot, as there was less chance of hitting a ball through someone's window when you are kicking it. One day I was home and there was no one around to play with. I had Barbie dolls but never played with them much, being more into outdoor sports. I had complained to my mother that there was no one around to play with, but she was busy vacuuming and told me to go play with my dolls. I went to my room and closed the door because of the noise. As I sat there staring at them, out of my peripheral vision a man a little bigger than I was appeared across from me up against the wall. He had a rumpled hat on, was pudgy, with a roundish face, dark hair and dark shiny eyes, and his clothes were brown. There was something about his eyes that was different, but I could not put my finger on it at the time but have since figured it out, he had no whites. He had this aura of power about him and was a bit scary at first. Upon seeing him I exclaimed, "Who are you and what are you doing in my room?" He said, "Didn't I just hear you wish you had someone to play with?" I looked at him for a moment, frowning. He was a stranger but his logic made sense to my innocent mind, I had said that. Even so, something felt strange, he was a grownup even though he was only my size, and they did not normally play with kids, so I asked him, "What can "You" play?" He pointed at the dolls and asked me what I did with them. I showed him how I could dress and undress them and pretend they were dancing. I was babbling away and my mother happened to be vacuuming the hall on the other side of my door and heard me talking. She yelled over the vacuum, "Janet who are you talking to?" I looked up at him and he shook his head and said, "Do not tell her." I did not feel right about not telling her and I said, "Why, she won't mind, we aren't doing anything wrong!" "She won't be able to see me," he said. I got tingles then, but told him that was silly, and he said, "If you tell her she will not let you play with me anymore and I will have to leave." Well this was a problem to me and I did not know what to do. On the one hand, I wanted to have a playmate, but knew I would have to tell my mother the truth. About that time she opened the door, which I was sitting in front of and stuck her head around the edge saying, "Who are you talking to?" I said, "Him" and nodded my head in his direction figuring he was right there and she would see him anyway. She looked right at him and said, "Who? Where, I don't see anyone?" I dropped my mouth open, looked at him and then back at her. How could he be right? I looked at her, said, "You don't see him", and turned back to point at him and he was gone. I jumped up, exclaiming, "Where did he go? Where'd he go?", and ran over to my window thinking he had jumped out of it, as that was the only other way out of the room. Even as I ran over to it I knew he had not gone out it as my mother would have seen him and he could not have gotten out it in time when I turned my head around. Now my mother was looking at me with a scared look on her face as if l was crazy. "You shouldn't talk like that Jahnets or they will lock you up." "But" I exclaimed, "he was right here."

My mother thought I had a vivid imagination and was lonely for a playmate so was pretending to have an invisible playmate. I heard about it again at the dinner table along with the rest of the family. Only he had not been invisible to me, and if l had made someone up, it more than likely would have been a kid like me not an adult brownie or leprechaun, especially when at the time I didn't even know what a brownie or leprechaun was. To this day, I am puzzled why this one came and was listening to me. I am pretty sure he was a brownie though. He was true to his word though and he never did come back.

Summer went on and sometimes my friends and I would go down to a creek a few blocks away to play. We went to the creek with other kids to catch skeeters, the bugs that looked like a big mosquito only they skied across water. Most kids caught Polly-wogs but our creek did not have any, only skeeters. I was in about third grade at the time and my mother did not like me down there out of sight, especially when I kept coming home with wet tennis shoes. She told me not to go down there any more that bums hung out down there and would get me. One day no one was around to play with and I could think of nothing to do and the creek popped into my head. I went to the creek and was squatting over the water waiting for the bugs to get closer so I could grab them. There was a brown root from one of the trees going down towards the water in front of me and I stood on it to avoid getting my shoes wet. My foot moved as if something moved under it and I looked down at the root to see if it was slipping out from under my foot.

As I looked at the root, I realized it looked sort of like a skinny pant leg and my eyes followed it upwards, it was looking more and more like a leg and I followed it up to look into the eyes of a man leaning back against the tree. I was so startled I jumped straight up, and he said, "Watch out, do not fall in the water". I stepped in the water and got one of my tennis shoes wet and glared at him as I jerked it out, thinking my mother would know I had been at the creek. "Where did you come from," I exclaimed. He looked intently at me and said, "Why did I scare you?" I was just starting to notice boys, and found it a little unnerving to have him ask me if he scared me because he was beautiful in a dark sultry way and my mother had warned me about strange men being down at the creek and he had startled me. Somehow he seemed to know this and that bothered me. Of course my mother did not really know there were bums hanging around or not, as she had never been down there. Then he said, "You should listen to your mother she knows what she is talking about."

Now this was getting strange, to have this guy just pop in out of nowhere and repeat my own thoughts of what she had said to me was unsettling, it seemed as if he was reading my mind. I asked him again where he came from and looked around trying to figure out how he could have possibly gotten so close to me without me even hearing him as there were only two ways in and out of there. I had literally been squatting on top of his leg, and it just did not make any sense to me. He was wearing a dark brown leather outfit that could fade right into the dirt, tree trunk and shadows, had long dark hair, and slightly almond eyes and he seemed completely oblivious to how beautiful he was. While I was looking him over he looked down or away as if listening for something. I asked him if he was a bum and he opened his mouth, looked at his clothes, and said, "Do I look like a bum?" I said, "No," but pointed out that his clothes were different from what I was used to seeing, more like what a Gypsy wore in the old western movies. Then he changed the subject and asked me what I was doing down there. I told him I was catching skeeters and he asked, "Why?" I told him because I was bored and had nothing to do. He made a comment about it not being nice for the bug, and made me feel bad, like because I was bored I was selfishly not thinking about the bug. I looked at him, and told him I let them go after I caught them and did not hurt them. He looked down at them to see this was true and then looked back at me and smiled slightly. Then he leaned back against the tree again, and said something that made the whole incident stick in my mind all this time.

He said, "You know he is going to be angry you are down here!" At first I thought he must mean my dad, but I did not think this guy knew my dad and asked, "Who is going to be angry?" He looked me in the eye and he said, "You know who." Strangely enough as I looked at him puzzled and the image and feeling of God came to me. I said, "Oh, he doesn't care about me", and the man became angry and for the first time and glanced around as if he were afraid someone had heard us. I was a little scared but at the same time there was something in his eyes that made me want to stand my ground. I stared back, chin out daring him to say something. Suddenly he grinned and his eyes softened and he looked past me and inward, like he was only just realizing that I was attracted to him and he did not want me to be and said you had better go now, as if I would not be safe if I stayed, and I said, "But", and he sternly said ''Now.'' At which I jumped to my feet and took three steps before I could stop my feet from moving on their own, and turned back to look at him and make sure he was still on the other side of the water and he was gone. I stopped and looked all around. It was impossible for him to have moved that fast. Then I felt really spooked. The energy of the place had changed to dark and scary and I left as fast as I could. I felt spooked all the way home and felt as though someone were right behind me, following me. I kept turning around looking back expecting to see someone there, but never did. Then I sat in my backyard thinking on what he had said for a long time, and what I was going to tell my mother about my wet shoes. He had made me move and take three steps before I could get back control and stop my body from moving, and I knew he had. The ramif Ications of this reverberated in my young mind for hours as I sat there. Finally I heard my mother yelling my name out the front door and looking down at my wet shoes answered, "I'm in the back yard."

When ever any of these meetings happened I would always think about them for a long time going over every detail trying to understand why it happened. I think because the energy of it was so different from any other feeling, and I could not say anything to anyone, as they never believed me when I did. So I tried to figure it out by myself, why the energy felt different, why they always seemed to dress different. It got to the point that I could tell when something was about to happen because I recognized the energy signature. There are beings that are more powerful than humans psychically, and just because they have these abilities does not mean they use them for evil purposes. But they do have a different type of energy and it tends to make most humans chakras open and feels very much like what you would think pheromones would do. Your adrenaline is apt to start pumping at the unknown feeling of it all, and I feel this is a fear humanity has to get over. Just like the saying that absolute power corrupts absolutely, it is just not true all the time. Some beings have honor that even though it is different from what humanity might think of as honor, it is still honor. Many teachers have made comments to me that some of your best teachers could be your worst enemies. After all it takes much more love to play the part of your enemy in life just so they can help you learn, than to play a friend who leads you astray. I am able to step aside from my fears about them being different, and see what they are doing or teaching me on another level. This also makes me a little more difficult to teach.

Chapter Three

While we lived at this house I also taught myself how to continue a dream the next night. I had a dream about a white stallion and I would imagine myself to be this horse. The dream would always have cowboys chasing the horse up and down hills trying to catch it, but they never could. I loved to run, and I loved horses so I would lie back down to go to sleep the next night and go back to the last thing in the dream I remembered from the night before and focus on it, I would suddenly be there continuing the dream. It was great and I did it over and over again for many nights. Finally one night I changed it and wondered what would happen if I let them catch me. It was bad then, I was corralled and could not get out, so I never had that dream again. I also had the same type of dream about Snidely Whiplash and Dudley Do Right, only this was not by choice. I was always saving someone or being tied to railroad tracks or a wood saw until I realized that they did not want to be saved or they would not allow them selves to be in that position time after time again. I remember yelling at this meek girl and telling her this and she just shrugged. I thought she was stupid and deserved to be on the tracks. Then I never dreamed it again.

Thinking back on this now I have to wonder if being tied to tracks and saws was how my mind dealt with being abducted, but then I learned from the dreams too. This recurring dream or other dreams where I ran into burning houses and saved people happened all during my life. It was not until just recently that I realized why. Sooner or later mother has to let go and let the grown kid either sink or swim on their own. Like the girl on the saw, I could not save her from her lessons, or herself. She had to learn them her way, and it is only the egos safety mechanism that makes the soul feel bad for the girl because the ego can not get past the fact that her body is getting hurt. This is because the ego is part of the body and it does not comprehend that her soul is learning from this how to stand up for herself, and more importantly how not to let others hurt themselves. I will point something else out here that I asked about and was just shown more of the answer, the ego is the son of

Hera (the earths soul) and Zeus (King of the gods/spirits), because we all have a spirit and a soul, and when it was prophesized that Zeus' son would take over from him, it came true. The ego has taken over this world and that is what is destroying it.

While I lived on the desert, my mother was always afraid that we would be bit by a rattlesnake or scorpion. I would always tell her that they could not get me because I was too fast for them and could jump too high. Later when we moved to the Bay Area this dream would haunt me. I had it repeatedly and it was more of a nightmare type that I did not want to have but somehow kept waking up consciously in. I would be on top of a hill in the desert, there were rattle snakes all over, and I had to run through them fast and jump so I would not be bit to get off the hill. The last time I had the dream, I made it past all the snakes to a clearing and stopped to look back thinking I had finally made it. I looked down, and another snake had snuck up behind me almost running if a snake could do this, and I was bit, and it woke me up it hurt so much. My father came in to see what was going on, I was crying, and rubbing my leg saying a snake had bit me.

He asked to see my leg and it was red where I was rubbing it, so he checked my bed thinking that maybe a spider bit me. I never had that dream again after it bit me. My father was interested in my dreams and asked me about it then. I told him about being able to fall back asleep and go back to the same part of a dream where I left off. My parents just thought I was really smart. My father was a genius, so they did not think anything unusual about it.

At school the boys would get mad at me for catching their fly balls during baseball or outdoing them in some sport. One time a boy hit a ball out to me on purpose because I had just walked up to the outfield with the remnants of my lunch in hand, and was trying to eat them quickly so I could play. I had a drink in one hand and a bag of chips in the other, and literally jumped straight up four feet to catch the ball and clasp it to me without a glove and with only a couple of fingers. It was hit so hard that when I jumped up in the air it hit me in the solar plexus and I held it to me but it also knocked me off my feet backwards and I landed flat on my back still trying not to drop anything. That was apparently the last straw for him, he came walking out to the out field and was hitting me with his glove when another friend stopped him saying he was a poor sport. For the next three weeks that boy and another of his friends harassed me after school. During school they would say they were going to beat me up and if l said anything to anyone I would get it worse. I just ran home after school and they could never catch me. Then it got to the point I did not want to go to school anymore, and my father noticed this. He asked me what was up and I told him. He went to the school and talked to the principal about it but was not satisfied with her answers so when he came home he pulled me out back and strapped boxing gloves on me and was teaching me how to box. Of course my mother had a conniption fit over my father teaching his daughter how to box, so he stopped. Then he told me that if I just kicked him between the legs if he came after me again that would stop him. I was in third grade when this happened and did not believe that was going to stop him. He guaranteed me it would stop him. So the next time he ran up behind me after school and grabbed my shoulder and spun me around I kicked as hard as I could. The poor boy was on the ground in seconds and I started running home. His friend then caught up with me on my block, and told me I was going to really get it now. Then a neighbor saw what was happening and told him to leave me alone and told me to run on home. I told my father what happened and he called the school again and we were all in the principals office the next day. All because a girl outdid a boy. It seemed like a constant battle for me just to get along with others.

We had been renting this house and that summer we moved to a new house three doors down from my grammar school, that my parents would buy. My father tore up the whole back yard with a rotor tiller and planted a vegetable garden. I helped him after school. I can still remember sitting in the only tree, a purple plum tree and eating plums and watching him water. It was hard to find something challenging to keep me busy so my father taught me chess and would play with me a couple of times a week, till I beat him. I picked it up quickly, and since he did not have anyone else to play with, he would play with me.

I also had a place to lay in the sun in our back yard at the new house, a pass time I loved to do. I would close my eyes and daydream and talk to my guardian angel or higher self.

Of course I did not realize I was doing this at the time. All I realized was that he cared about me and it made me feel loved and protected. I have always felt protected like someone was watching over me.

I must have seen a Tarzan show, or maybe a Shirley Temple movie that had a voodoo witch doctor in it and I can remember thinking that it made sense how it worked. I somehow realized that the doll did not have to look like the person. It had to do with belief, you had to believe the doll was the person, then what ever you did to the doll also would happen to the person. One day shortly after this, a boy at school that I had a crush on said something hurtful to me about my red hair in front of our mutual friends. He alluded to the woman that lived across the street from the school who had one child with brown hair and one with red and one with black, while she had red and her husband was blondish red. It had embarrassed me and made me feel like I would never be accepted because I had red hair. He seemed to feel this made me a bad person and it was the first time I had ever heard this about red hair. I was so angry I went home and lay on my bed sobbing. My teddy bear lay there and I thought I'll fix him. I got some needles from my sewing kit and stuck one in the head and one in the gut and one in the arm, all the while visualizing this boy. Right about that time my father must have heard me crying and knocked on my door. I threw the teddy bear under my bed then and forgot about it. I told him what happened and said I wanted to have my hair dyed another color. He became really angry then. He said he knew kids could be mean about any trait a person had that they felt was not perfect, but that I had beautiful hair and someday men would be falling all over themselves just to meet me. He said just the right thing I needed to hear and gave me hope that someday I would be accepted. My father and I were kindred spirits. It was about three days later that I noticed I had not seen the boy who had made these remarks. I wanted to tell him my daddy thought I was beautiful and now because of his hateful remarks I would not even look at him sideways when I was older. Unfortunately, I had not seen him anywhere to tell him this. I finally asked a mutual friend where he was, and was told he had been sick and that they had taken him to the Doctors office but they could not figure out what was wrong with him. It was at this moment I remembered the Teddy Bear still hidden under my bed with the needles still in it. I had forgotten all about it after I did it. I spent the rest of the day thinking it could not possibly be the bear, this was all in my imagination. I went home after school and retrieved the bear and took the needles out, hoping that the kid would be ok. Miraculously he was at school the next day. I never tried Voodoo again. For some reason I could not explain it seemed to work for me, so I was not going to chance it again. After all revenge belonged to God and I did not want to get in trouble doing his job.

That coming summer I went to summer school and for some reason completely unknown to me at the time, I chose two classes that were real work. Now most kids will pick Art or something easy, as it is supposed to be summer and they really do not want to be in school during vacation, and I was no different. Public speaking and Greek and Roman history were my first choices, and I even remember thinking I would get a head start on next year, and you know they gave them both to me. I still remember being notif Ied that my first choices where the classes I would be taking and sitting there looking at the paper wondering, "What had I been thinking." Even my mother laughed at me when I told her they had given me both of my first choices, which they never did. I wrote my first term paper on the Greek and Roman Gods and found I could not get enough of them. I read their stories repeatedly all summer even after class was out, trying to understand why Hera would do something, or Zeus. My teacher was Mr. Johnson and as it turned out, in fifth grade I had him again for a regular teacher. He challenged me and seemed to have faith in me. One day he was teaching us some form of math leading us up to algebra. He asked a simple question. Too simple I thought. and though he had asked something like what is two times two, I answered 2,4.6,8,10,12 and so on. I do not remember exactly what he asked us, all I remember is I answered him like, "Yeah, yeah." He thought I did not understand him and said, "No," and turned to ask another student. Then slowly he turned back to me and said, "Jahnets all this time I thought you just did not understand what I was saying to you, and you have been so far ahead of me that I was the one that could not understand you." At the next parent teacher conference, he told my mother I should be tested for a high IQ. I was not tested until I took the California State tests before 6th grade. All the students knew the day before about the tests that we were having them and I just decided I was going to try this time and see how well I could do for myself. Well they pulled my parents in the principals' office a few days later wondering if l had cheated and told them I had the IQ of a genius. They would not tell me how high it was because my mother was afraid it would go to my head, only that it was genius range and they wanted to know if l wanted to be moved up into 7'11 or maybe 8th grade. This idea scared me as I had finally made a few friends. I wanted to stay with the friends I had made and so passed it up. After that, any teachers I came into contact with always said they thought I could do better no matter what work I had done. One more way to be different was all I saw in this. It seemed like I was always too smart for my own good, or thought I was too pretty, or was too good at sports or something else, so that I never felt accepted for me.

I always dreamed lucidly, at least the dreams I remember I do. I would wake up in dreams often and have to figure out where I was and then realize I was in a dream. It was in doing this that I learned some of what was really happening in our dreams. I woke up in one and there were four or five people standing around me. I do not remember what the dream was about but I remember looking the people in the eye, and when I spoke to them all but one looked like a store dummy of the person I was speaking to with blank eyes, even though they spoke back to me just like normal. The one that was lucid or conscious I realized was really there with me, and the others were like props. This scared me at first as I also realized that the one that was there with me was not really who they appeared to be and had some control. Who ever it was realized that I realized this and after that the one that was there with me would look like someone I did not know but was there for a logical reason. I could always tell which ones were really in the dream with me, because when I looked into their eyes they looked back. I also realized that I would learn more if they did not know I was lucid, since then I could watch them. So I would fake it like I had not noticed so I could watch and see what was really going on, and discovered them watching me. I had to not look them in the eye though because then they would read me and know that I knew, and then I would wake up. There are many different kinds of dreams is what I discovered. Sometimes I would wake up partially from a dream and not know where I was and walk back to my parents room or my older sisters room afraid. Thinking back on this now, maybe I was being taken and it was their energy signature I felt upon waking that scared me.

My older sister and her boyfriend would drive up to Stinson Beach sometimes and would take me with them. This beach is North of the Bay Area on Highway 1 and the road to get there is all curves around the coast. It is a very beautiful drive and a sandy beach instead of rocks. One day on the way there, I had already been admonished not to be a backseat driver and so, was trying not to say anything. As we came around a curve, I could see across a gorge to where the road continued. There was another car coming our way. As most young drivers having fun, he was taking the curves on the inside. I tried to say something about the other car I had seen coming, but was admonished to be quiet. Then when we got down to the hairpin turn my sisters' boyfriend Joe, was taking it on the inside wrong lane and the other car just so happened to be doing the exact same thing from the opposite direction only they were in the out side lane on the curve. I do not think I have ever seen two cars change lanes and miss each other so fast in my life. After passing, each other they both pulled over to find their stomachs and I made the mistake of saying, "Didn't you see him?" Both he and my sister turned around and said, "You saw him coming and did not say anything?" I said, "Well you guys told me to shut up and sit there or I wouldn't be able to come again." There was nothing he could say, and my sister had her hand over her mouth and just shook her head to be quiet. Finally, a little later he turned around and said, "From now on you say so if you see a car coming, no matter what we have said." I told him ok. I mention this because I have had many hairy experiences that logic states should have been accidents, but somehow turned out not to be. In fact this ability seems to run in my family since the one instance my mother told me about my fathers abilities he was doing the same thing. He and my mother had gone out with another couple and were coming back across the bay bridge at night. On the bottom level there is a sharp turn towards the Richmond side right before the bridge ends. My father kept telling their friend to slow down, even though he was not going too fast to begin with. As they came around that comer there was a large pile up of cars that they would have been in had he continued at that speed. We should always listen to our intuition, always.

There was a couple that I saw in a dream around this period of time that were in a ship. At least I thought it was a dream. The man was shorter than the woman and wore glasses and had long hair. He looked hobbit like, hat and all. The woman looked like Brunhilda with blonde hair and was his assistant and much taller than him. He was a scientist or doctor and knew a lot about herbs. I remember him saying to me that I would have a problem with my back someday because of something. One night as I was falling asleep I thought of this couple. I always felt like they really cared for me. I woke in a lucid dream walking with others in a forest in the dark. It was really dark but I could see a ship sitting in a gorge hidden from view behind a hill. All of us entered the ship and I went towards the left in another direction from them down a hall. At the time I do not know how I knew where to go but I did. As I walked the darkened hall it felt really scary as if something were there with me and I hurried to a door and opened it and ran inside. There they were and I hugged him and said hi to his assistant across the room. He turned me around and checked my back again and seemed to feel it was doing fine but I had to be careful with it. Then he told me I could leave and I told him it was scary outside his office and asked him to walk me out. He told me he did not have time to walk me out but if I walked straight out and did not look around I should be fine. Not wanting to seem like a baby, I left. As I walked down the hall I could see the door leading to the outside as there was moonlight outside. Then I heard a noise and looked to my left. There were many beings laying along the side of the hall way as if there were not enough beds and they were laying around trying to sleep or were sick. As I stared at what one day I would know are grays, one of them very irritated said, "What are you staring at? Weren't you told to not look around and just leave?" As he said this he leaned over in my direction rather threateningly so that his face was clearer. Now I was scared but somehow I worked up the nerve to frown at his rudeness and say, "You! I have never seen anyone like you before." He looked like he hurt and was grumpy from lack of sleep and it seemed as though they were all hanging around in this corridor because they had not enough room on board. I asked him if he were ok. Then he softened a little and said, "Then you better move on and do what you were told to." I ran out of the ship with my feelings hurt, and it was early morning as the light was beginning to come up and it was not as dark as it had been. I was in a forest somewhere and turned and looked one last time at the ship as I was walking along a path and then...

When I had these dreams I would always wake and there was a buzzing sound as I woke like I had just been transferred into my body. I believe this couple were the grays that had originally taken me, and where to me this was real, I was always assured by my mother it was a dream. She always said it as though I was stupid to question whether it was a dream or not and others in the family would agree with her and laugh at me, making me feel silly to think otherwise. I was considered by them to have a vivid imagination.

Chapter Four

Meanwhile my parents started having problems between them partly because of the insecurity my fathers illness caused in him and the tranquilizers they gave him to keep him calm so his vein would not burst again. Years later they would take these tranquilizers off the market because they made people mean and belligerent. My father had gone from being in the Air Force and being a pilot, gunner and Master Sergeant, to not being able to find a job because of his illness and it made him very angry and insecure as the head of the family. After many years of arguments they ended up getting a divorce. My dad moved out and lived about four blocks away in an apartment and my younger sister and I would go see him every weekend. One day I was sitting out front a friend's house on the grass with about six other kids. It was a week or so before Halloween and the minister from our church came over. I saw him park and go to our door. The older kids told me

I should go and see what is up. I told them I was afraid to, that he was there to tell my mother that my dad had died. They looked at me with their mouths open, not believing I had just said that and asked me if I wanted my father to be dead. "No of course not", I exclaimed. "Then why don't you go see?" he said, himself being the curious one. At that moment, my mother called me home. After the minister told me, I asked if I could go back with my friends. My mother was not sure if I should because she knew how close I was to my father, but the minister thought that might be comforting to me, so she let me leave. My friends could not believe I was right, and kept asking me how I knew. The friend who had been curious felt awful now, and I told him it was not his fault. Just a feeling was all I could say, as I did not know how I knew, I just knew. The truth was when they had asked what I thought he was there for, that was the answer that had come to my mind, and I had just blurted it out as surprised as they were that I had said it. This blurting things out has happened many times through out my life so that I have to stop and be on guard constantly that I will not say something that will make people feel scared of me. Most people can not handle it if they think someone can read their mind and will challenge me saying things like, "You don't know that." Or "Prove it." I learned sometime along the way that people have secrets and it was not for me to reveal them all.

One thing the minister had wanted was for us to continue coming to his church even though my mother and my aunt were not on speaking terms at the time. The next time we went my mother asked me if I wanted to go with her to the Ladies meeting after the main sermon. I thought this was great as it made me feel all grown up even though I was only in 7th grade. The following Sunday our minister gave a meaningful sermon about loving one another. It really touched me in a way none had before and I felt like Jesus was there with me. After the sermon, everyone split up to go to their respective meetings, for kids, women and men. I walked around the room full of women, said, " Hello" to a few, then came back, and stood next to my mother. As I stood there listening, I noticed that they all seemed to be talking about someone, gossiping about what they were wearing or who they were talking to. I could not believe that after that wonderful sermon about loving one another and being kind to one another, they were standing there gossiping about people. It seemed so hateful to me and I was so disappointed in them. I finally said something to my mother and the woman next to her heard me. She chuckled and raised her eyebrows at my mom, who said I think we had better leave now. After we left, I was admonished for embarrassing her in the woman's group. I began crying and told her I never wanted to go back there. They did not care about what the minister said, I was young, and idealistic felt we should be trying to change and do better at the very least while we were there in church. To me we were in the house of God and these women could not even stop back stabbing others while they were there. I was young and did not realize at the time that most people see chmch as a social occasion, a chance to dress up and meet with their neighbors and friends and raise money or have a potluck. I saw it as a time to listen to the ministers words and look deep within myself and see what needed to be changed within me. Where all this idealism came from I know now, and it was there from the very beginning. My first heroin was Isis. I can remember watching one of the first TV shows when

I was young on the desert and it being about a wonder woman type who saved people and I wanted to be like her. Strangely, I have never heard anyone else mention this show and I have to wonder if it was something played for me by the grays. There was one other show that I found when I researched this dming the same time period, but this woman wore a leopard print and I remember another type of outfit more like a Greek Goddess.

My mother worked full time then, so my sisters and I would clean and cook dinner for everyone. I would come home from school and vacuum, do the dishes from breakfast and start dinner. Sometimes I would go back over to the school and play football with the guys out front. I have always been able to watch something one time and then try it myself and usually was able to do it perfectly. This time while playing football, one of my male friends was six foot tall and came up in front of me, laughing to himself thinking I would not be able to get past him. To this day I am not sme why I did this, but I grabbed his hands and rolled backwards sitting down at the same time and putting my foot in his chest and threw him over my head. I then continued to run down the area we were using hearing his screams behind me and everyone else had to stop playing to laugh. I had seen it done in a cartoon and figmed it would work. It did.

One night I was woke up in the middle of the night. I looked around the room I shared with my sister and at the foot of my bed, it looked like someone was standing in the shadows. I have always had pretty good night vision and could make out a form. I closed my eyes and looked again and still I could see this form. It seemed to have horns so I thought it was the devil. I must have picked this up from a science fiction show but I believed if I did not believe in him, he would not exist. I would not be giving him any power over me. So I said," Go Away, I don't believe in you". He disappeared. The next morning it did not look like anything but clothes on a bench, and no matter which angle I looked at them there was no way it even remotely looked like a devil. I thought it had worked. For most of my life, I have had thoughts that ended up in reality. I cannot explain why I knew what you believe becomes reality other than things had happened since I was a child that pointed to this and I was smart enough to notice them even if l had not figured it out exactly. To me it was magic. I was not quite sure how to make it work, but I knew it had to do with what I believed. Sometimes I would half wake from a dream but not be all the way back, and I remember walking down the hall and standing next to my mothers bed because I was not sure where I was and was looking for someone familiar. I can remember doing this many times and she just thought I was walking in my sleep, only I was awake, it was just that where I was did not look right.

The summer of eighth grade, I met what would be my first husband and fell in love. Of course, I would not know we would be married until much later, but it was love at first sight.

Then my mother was remarried and we had to move to Seattle. I was devastated but had no choice but to move. When we were almost to Seattle, the trees started getting really thick and dark. Like what you would think the black forest in Germany looks like. Scary like the kind of forest you do not want to get lost in. My stepfather and mother bought a house just north of Ravenna Park in Seattle. Ninth grade was spent at a new school where the attitudes were completely different from Northern California. It also snowed. My first winter season a girl came to school that had hit a tree skiing the first week of snow. Other than two cute guys who had to help her get around, she had casts on both her legs and one arm. I did not think I wanted to learn to ski since there were many trees around then. Society was much more conservative in Seattle than California. The people were not as openly friendly, I think now because of lack of sun. Back then they did not like Californians coming to their state, because they wanted to keep it nice. New people meant change. I was in culture shock. I had come from a school that was mixed racially with Caucasian only being 5% to an area where most of the kids were Caucasian and came from rich or well to do families. I still did not fit in but I did make two new friends that year. Then during summer, two weeks before tenth grade I met Dan. Dan had a friend who liked one of my friends and the whole first half of 10th grade was great. I was in love and had friends.

During physical education, I excelled in high jump, long jump and hurdles. One day during PE, most of the class went out on the field except for three other girls and myself. We were practicing our standing high jumps inside. Someone had given big chunks of foam to the school to make it softer when we hit the mats only they were oblong chunks and too big, so that if you stepped on the edge you would loose balance and could twist your ankle. We were trying to see how high we could go doing the scissors over the bars and because all four of us were good, and we kept moving the bar up. We raised the bar up to somewhere between four foot eight inches and five foot, I went over with my right foot and then my left foot hit the bar and threw me off balance and knocked the bar off, I landed on the foam twisting my right ankle, and then the bar in the midst of falling hit my ankle on the other side. I tore two ligaments and sprang it bad. My teacher was out on the field and another teacher came in and put ice on it. I screamed. The ice hurt worse but she kept insisting on it. Finally, my teacher came in. We could not get my parents on the phone and all I wanted was to go home, so I walked and ended any Olympic hopes for me. A week later, I told my mother I needed to go to the Doctor as it was turning colors and still hurt. They put me in a splint and taped it up it was so bad. Shortly after this, I broke up with my first boyfriend, Dan. He was older and my mom did not like him because he smoked so I could never talk to him on the phone. It was a bad winter.

The next spring was great. I had new friends at high school and had made it through the winter gray months of the Pacif Ic North West. Ravenna Park became a major hang out for all of us. There was a rope swing off a bridge and we would go there a lot swinging and partying. One couple for some reason could not see each other anymore and were madly in love. They decided to have a marriage in the open air in the park. We found an old wagon half buried in the woods and pulled it out into a glade. There were cases of beer and weed was being passed around. It was 1969 and war protests and sit ins and love ins were the scene. After hearing their vows to each other, I could see how much they loved each other in their eyes and I thought to myself, I wonder if l will ever love someone as much as they obviously love each other. No sooner had I thought the words than a person ran past my line of sight and into the clearing, seemingly out of nowhere. He seemed to come out of thin air and no one seemed to notice this but me as I had been looking in that direction when he just appeared and I followed him with my eyes into the glade.

I stared at him and could not take my eyes off him. He had curly golden hair and blue eyes. He noticed me sitting on the wagon staring, and I turned away blushing. This was not like me at all to just blatantly stare, and I was embarrassed that I could not stop staring at him for some reason. Then he came and sat by me and we talked. He was from the east coast and was visiting a friend in town. He was about to start college and had come to check out the University of Washington. He was interested in philosophy. He asked me why I was down there and said I should not be there as it was dangerous for a girl. That set me off. I told him what is good for the goose is good for the gander and he became irritated. He asked me what I wanted from him, and much to my surprise I said, "Kiss me." He was so surprised I asked that he did. Afterwards he said, "Well, can you tell?" I asked what he meant and he said, "Weren't you thinking you can tell by his kiss?" That made me laugh because I had been thinking something of the sort, and said, "What you mean you can not tell?" We both laughed. We talked for a while after that and then he ran off the way he had come. Neither of us would remember each other as being this person the next time we met. That would not be for about seven years. In the meantime, much would happen.

The one and only protest I ever walked in was in Seattle. It was protesting the war in Vietnam. It was suppose to be peaceful and to walk along a certain road, but as we walked past an entry to the express way a man that was out in front with us tried to get the crowd riled up enough to try and shut down the express way. I have never liked trouble makers and this guy looked completely sinister to me. I stood up to him and said he was a trouble maker and that is what was causing all the trouble between the police and the protesters lately, since they were only doing their job. He got angry and came towards me and two other women told him if he laid one hand on me they would have him jailed. He ran off like he did not want to run into the police and the rest of the march went peaceful like it was suppose to be. I have always felt like he had been sent there to get the protestors to be disruptive on purpose, and if that was why I was there. To stand up to him and stop him.

Every year on my birthday for many years I would go horseback riding. This year we were in Seattle and the closest place was in Issaquah. It was rainy, muddy and the horses did not want to be out of their warm stall. I was riding on a beautiful black Morgan gelding. We began riding and my bridle came loose somehow and cut his mouth when I pulled it to stop him, and then broke off so I only had one lead. This spooked the horse and he took off down a path partially overgrown, at a dead run. I was holding on for dear life when I saw a puddle about 6 feet long ahead of us and felt the horse bunch up ready to jump and flew over the puddle. It was all I could do to hold onto the horn. Finally I reached down and grabbed the lead and used it for the other side of the reins and slowed him down and walked him into the barn area. I have always wondered if that horse was a Phooka as I had never had a horse take off like that before.

It may have been the wild ride on what I termed the Phooka but more than likely it was just time for me to learn more. I began having dreams of flying where I would just take off from the ground and not know how to land. I had many dreams like this. One I remember was where a whole town of people were chasing me because I could fly. They kept getting in my way when I tried to land so I finally jetted ahead of them and landed. Of course this could have been in reference to my teenage partying also, but I have always found it interesting that it was towns people who would not let me come down. Life went on normally for a while then I had a lucid dream about destruction in Seattle. It looked like a war zone everywhere. I was in a skirt and sandals, it was a fall evening, and I was walking up a hill and it was cold and damp. I remember looking at my shoes and thinking this would happen when it was getting cold and I had sandals on. Then I got to a white brick house that was caved in on a hill. There were police out front trying to keep a crowd from going in. I ran around them and headed towards the side of the house. The officer stopped me and I pulled out of his hands and said, "I have to get my son." I ran around the side and came out with a boy. I was lucid in the dream and it shocked me that I had said that. I looked closely at him since I did not have any children at the time, and that woke me up. I knew from that time on that I would have a boy first, and I did much later. My parents also bought that house many years later and lived there for a long time and there was a door around the back side where I had gone in my dream. The front had large windows and it was sunken from the sidewalk. It was white brick. Now some people say that remote viewing does not work, but having a lucid dream where your consciousness is awake in the dream to me is the same thing as remote viewing. The only difference is during remote viewing you are going somewhere specif Ically to see something or someone and in a lucid dream you simply wake up in the dream and really had no conscious choice of where you wake up or are going.

I worked at a restaurant waitressing during the second half of tenth grade. One day I made it to work early and was standing out front the restaurant. A huge tiger swallowtail butterfly came floating by me and I instinctively put my hand out. It landed on my finger and stayed there for about five minutes much to the amazement of the cars driving by. Finally a couple walked up from the other direction about to walk into the restaurant and the woman saw the butterfly and said, "Is that a real butterfly?" I said, "Yes", and slowly they walked over to me to see. When they came too close to me, the butterfly took off and they groaned. "Ah well" I stated, "Butterflies are free."

Chapter Five

I hung out at the park across the street after work with friends there. There were a lot of people that hung out there during nice weather. A group of them were going camping up in eastern Washington and I was asked if I wanted to go. It sounded like fun and one of the guys I knew from school that was a friend, had a van and said he would drive if I wanted to go. So we went. We met at the Lake and regrouped with a few others who needed rides and left. On the way up a guy who looked just like my first love began paying attention to me. We talked all the way up there. He reminded me so much of my first boyfriend it was surprising to me. It was like he was a twin. He said he had just broken up with his wife a few weeks earlier and I laughed at him. He stated it was true and asked another girl I knew if it was true and she agreed. I was young and naYve about how truly traitorous men and other jealous girls can be and fell for it.

Maybe I wanted to because he looked so much like my first love, I do not know now. It took about four hours to get up there, and we locked up the van and walked up to see where we were camping. While I was on my way back to the van he stopped me and we walked off the trail and found a spot to talk and get to know each other. We began making out and one thing lead to another and we ended up in his sleeping bag in this little clearing off away from everyone else.

Everything was fine until we heard a crashing coming through the woods and his friend shows up with four other guys saying something about now it was his turn and they were buddies and shared everything. I looked at the guy I was with and he did not say anything and so I told his friend to go jump in the lake. The guy I was with jerked my arm and said, "That's not nice." I looked at him and in that moment I realized that even though he looked like my frrst love he was no where near him. There was no honor in this man and I felt thoroughly betrayed. I said, "Well it's not happening here." He actually looked at me angrily and said, "Who is going to stop it?" I said, "I am." He laughed and said, "Oh really and how are you going to do that?" I was so angry and felt so betrayed that for a split second the thought entered my mind to suck the life force out of him and take his soul somehow knew I could do it and that he really deserved it.

Then I thought, no I do not want this poison in me, so I did the next best thing. I began giving him every bit of negativity I had collected in my 16 years, everything that was black or evil or bad. I saw it crawling back up him and flowing into him as I stared into his eyes. He suddenly in a small voice managed to get out, "What are you doing, what are you?" I did not answer at frrst, just kept sending all the blackness I could fmd in me into him. Again he said, "What are you?" Fear was creeping into his voice and the other guys could hear it. Then I said, "You don't know, do you?" He jumped out of the sleeping bag and ran off into the woods, and then I turned towards his friend and with one look he too ran off followed by the other four. I straightened myself up and went back to the larger group. It was quite obvious I was upset and a Native American friend I knew, Madon asked me what was wrong. I told him what had happened and he went to have a talk with the guy. He told me to sit down there with them and they would watch out for me. So I did. Still I was quite humiliated and it had ruined the whole trip. Why are men such pigs sometimes. I saw the guy who had driven us up there and asked him if it was possible to get a ride back? He told me he would be glad to but someone had stolen everything including all our food and sleeping bags and ripped all the wiring out of his van so it was not going anywhere. That really made the day. So we sat down and watched others flit around getting ready for the evening. My friend Maden got an extra sleeping bag out and gave it to me to use, and shared his food with us. I was furious though and knew that the other guy had had something to do with it. Then something really strange happened. Maden came up to me all concerned saying there were UFO's over by Johns van. I asked him what he was talking about and he looked at me and said, "Did you call them?", "Are they here because of you?" I still was not quite sure what was going on and said, "Call who, with what?" "What is going on?" He said, "There are two flying saucers over the rise by Johns van and are shining lights on it like they are looking for someone or something." I looked down then, and again he bent over and looked me in the eye and asked me if I had called them. I looked at him and said, " I do not know." "I'm pretty upset, maybe they can pick up on it somehow." Another guy there that was a friend named Larry asked, "Have you ever seen flying saucers before?" I told him yes and a few stories about things I had seen when I was younger. It was not the kind of stories Madon wanted to hear while out camping though and asked me to not talk about it, since what I had done was already making it around the camp and people were getting scared. Apparently the guy I had been with had already told everyone that I had done something to him and put a curse on him. No one was sure whether to believe them or not but it made them nervous about me. Maden though, being a native had a little more experience with strange events, abilities and beings. The strange thing is that on one level I knew somehow they were there because of me and at the same time was going through life denying it because it was too incredible to believe. When and if I did consider it and spoke to someone else about it, I was looked at as if I thought I was a god or something and laughed at.

The rest of the trip was uneventful and I was just grateful to get home. When I went to walk off, Maden stopped me and after everyone else left, he sat down with me and talked to me about what had happened. He seemed to think that by choosing to give him all the negative things in me I had given him my strength. I assured him I did not think I had, but there was no way I wanted his life force in me. He laughed at that, understanding my feelings. He wanted to know if I was going to report it to the police because he was afraid of getting some of the people there in trouble. I said, "No, I think it has been taken care of, he got what he deserved. He was attempting to hurt and poison me and instead poisoned himself by his actions. I do not feel guilty about it as he had no honor and I was defending myself." Then he said, "Well just don't get mad at me ok?" I laughed at that. I was to find out that somehow honor flew out the window when it came to men and sex in many cases. Two weeks later another guy I knew asked me if I wanted to go to the miniature golf course with him. He picked me up and we drove over by the lake to see if anyone was around that might want to join us before going on. He stopped behind a restaurant and I saw a girl come out and walk over to his car on my side. She was the wife of the guy that had done that to me and wanted to know why I was going out with her husband. I looked at her and then at my date so he knew that I knew he was treacherous, and told her I was sorry, that he did not deserve her and that I had been told both by him and another girl who she happened to know that they had broken up weeks before. I asked her why she was still with him when he did her that way. He had managed to make her feel like no one else would want her. I told her she was pretty and I was sure many other guys would want her. I told her that her husband had no honor and what he had done. I told her if she did not believe me she could ask Madon. Then I told the guy driving since he had no honor either that I was getting out there and left and walked home. He had not been there camping, but had believed the worst of me from others. I had been young and dumb and out of love for someone that I thought at the time I would never see again had fallen for scum, only to have many other people rub it in who did not know or understand the truth of what had happened. Only that I had been with a guy who lied and was married, and had others lie for him too, and that was supposed to be my fault.

I saved enough money to take a bus to California during the summer of 11th grade and decided to stay and live with my older sister. She had received her Masters in Psychology at the University of California, Berkeley. The house she was renting was partially furnished and her friend had left Tarot cards there in the book case. I learned how to read Tarot cards while living with her and discovered they really do work. The reason is because your spirit already knows the answers, so when you shuffle the deck, thinking and focusing on what you want to know, the cards will line up for your answer. While I was living with her there I would see the first love of my life again, begin dating and end up getting married a few years later.

It was nice being back in California and hooking up with old friends. One of my best friends was Roxi. I had known Roxi since 2nd grade and we had great times together. One of our favorite pastimes was driving around, and she taught me how to drive on the back roads in her mothers Lincoln. Mini road trips is what we did for fun, dragging the main to see who was there and what everyone was up to. Richmond the city we had grown up in was known for it's main street, and every Friday it would be crowded with souped up cars as they drove down the four or five blocks, light to light, and showed off. One evening we drove by a corvette only to see an old couple driving it down the main. We laughed and I remembered another friend I had showed me a picture of her grandmother from the back in a swimsuit. She had red hair too and from the back she looked twenty five and she was 80. I thought that was great irony and thinking that it would be funny to have red hair still when I was old and drive down the street and have young boys tum to look and find an old woman. I found the irony funny. A few years later I would ask my guide if I could have red hair until I died for just that reason, and he said "Yes." I still do not die my hair.

A few years later, we were driving down a street in my car and this young man came flying the opposite direction at us taking up most of the street. This person had been doing this to many people, playing chicken is what we called it back then. It irritated a lot of people, but ego that he was, he just kept doing it. I was fed up with it. Without a word, I sped up and drove up my side of the street towards the car. At the last possible moment my left hand moved the wheel slightly on it's own about a half an inch to the right. Our cars flew by each other with not much more than an inch between us, and I glared at him out the window. I could have reached over and smacked him we were so close. When it was over, Roxi asked me very calmly to pull over. I did and she got out of the car and kissed the ground. I had never seen her afraid before. She yelled at me wanting to know what I was doing. I said, "I do not know, but I bet that guy never does that to anyone else again." I told her about my hand moving on it's own and we decided I had a great guardian angel and I was lucky I did. As far as I know, I was right and that person never did do it to anyone again. I was to find out that in some strange way I had this ability to teach people lessons that they would remember only it was not me doing it, it was my spirit.

Another friend was Dawn and we three would get in the most philosophical discussions for eighteen year olds. We believed in reincarnation and the three of us made a pack that who ever died first would come back and tell the other two that there was an after life. Even back then I was trying to get the truth.

Then I was married and after six months of sitting home and taking care of a house I began wondering what I was going to do with the rest of my life. It was during this time, that I saw Uri Geller on TV, bending spoons. I had been wondering what I was going to do with my life. Why I was here? When he came on TV, even though I was highly skeptical at the time I thought I am going to find out if this is baloney or not. So I started reading everything I could get my hands on about the Philosophy, Occult, Meditation, Astrology, Numerology and anything else similar. I could not get enough of it. I was working at a fabric store and reading on the bus to and from work. I was reading about meditation one day and thought it would be nice if there were a group I could go to, and learn this with in a group setting so I would know if what I was doing was correct. Ask and you shall receive. A week later someone came into the fabric store with a flyer about a class in the valley. I joined. My first teacher, Corine was a psychic and worked with the police on cases. We had loads of fun at classes and she taught us about everything we wanted to know about. During my classes with Corine, we were meditating for a couple of hours once a week. We learned about chakras and wrapping as well as psychometry, the vibrations of objects and finding them when they are lost, telepathy, and she introduced us to our guides among other things. Some people had grays for guides. For others they would appear as a Saint or someone whom they were more relaxed. At first, all I could see was his hands and then a man with long golden hair. I thought he was John the Baptist. Then I began feeling like so many could not have the same guides and mine began showing up in a hooded cape. When I asked his name, he said I could call him Prometheus and after the first few months, he appeared as a gray. Judy had shown us how to find out if our guide was really our guide and if they were evil or not by asking them to help you hurt someone. If they agreed you did not want to be around them and should ask for help to get rid of them.

I had met a girl on the bus going to work who was into Astrology and began learning about that. I bought many books and could not get enough of it. I did my own chart by hand and studied it . Then I did my friends charts and compared. I also studied numerology. I was searching for my reason for being, my path and what I was here for.

One day I was watching something on T.V. and they were talking about abductees thinking they had an implant in them so that the aliens could find them. I sat there thinking about this for a while. I was pretty sure that what had happened to me as a child and my gray guide now were related, but I was also still at the stage where even though these thoughts run through your mind, once you focus on them or acknowledge them there is no turning back, so you keep trying to talk yourself out of it. You can not undo knowledge. I figured that if they could find us through this so called implant, that if I had one, I should be able to trace it backwards to them.

Go ahead and laugh, but I thought it was worth a try and had no one around to tell me it could not be done. So I turned off the T.V., and pulled my legs up and dropped into meditation. First I wrapped myself like my teacher had shown me, knowing that this would protect me. Then I blanked my mind of all thought and began looking for a cord. I reasoned it would have to travel like electricity back to it's source. There it was and I followed it. Suddenly a ship was coming into view in front of me and I was approaching it from the front right forward side from the occupants perspective. I was floating around outside the ship, watching two grays sitting at the controls. The one on the right hand side suddenly looked up and out the window there where I was floating and stared at me. I thought, "Hello." For a split second he just starred at me to the point I was not sure if he could even see me or if I was just imagining it all. Then quite suddenly he was in my mind and I flew off the couch and was freaking out running through the house screaming at the top of my lungs, "What the hell are you, you blanketie blank." I fmally managed to grab a door jam and stop myself and at the same time slapped a hand over my mouth to stop the obscenities that were still issuing from me. I stood there quite wide eyed for sometime, not believing what had just happened. Both upset that I had freaked so, thinking that had been my own fears coming out that I was not in control of somehow, and sad that at my first instance of contact with my friend had gone so haywire. I really thought it had been me saying all those things and I had totally blown first contact in my eyes. I cried. I did not talk to him for a couple of weeks and I thought he would never forgive me for what I had said. Then one day he came to me again and I apologized and he explained to me it had been him. I had snuck up on him when humans were not suppose to be able to do that. No one had ever done that to him and I had completely caught him off guard. After that our relationship became much more solid and when ever I did not understand something he would help me to understand, but only if I did not tell others. He was very concerned that I would attract attention of what he termed, "The Others," and I would end up a guinea pig.

I was reading, "Kundalini, the evolutionary energy in man", by Gopi Krishna. It was a heavy reading book, the kind of book where you would read a paragraph, and then would have to reread it to comprehend the feelings he was trying to portray. This was both because he was from another country where things were different and they spoke a different English, and because his energy had raised and so understood life differently than those of us who had not raised our energy. It took me some time to read it and during this time I had to throw out all of the references to it being dangerous, or that only men could accomplish this, or any other things that just did not feel right to me. People put most of these things in books I felt to protect themselves from being sued. See I really believe that if you believe it, it is true for you in some way and so those thoughts can also hold you back. Finally, one day I sat down in the middle of my living room alone. I went into deep meditation with the intention of making Kundalini rise. It felt like a snake inside of me crawling up my spine. It actually felt like I had something else alive inside me and I almost stopped when it had rose to my third chakra. I say this because it really does feel that way, and it took a lot of courage and faith for me to continue. It stopped briefly at my gut level Chakra and I knew I had to let go and not worry about whether I would live or die and just have faith. When I did, it rose completely to my crown and exploded in light. As I sat there aglow, a voice came to me after what seemed like a long time and said, "If you do not stop now you will die." I was too absorbed in the love and oneness I was feeling. I was with God, who wants to leave that? The voice repeated itself and somehow it got through. I realized it was talking about my ego or my body and that I needed them to go on in this physical life. With much reluctance, I let go and came back. I sat there for I do not know how long, almost not remembering how to move or if I even could. I can still remember looking at my legs and thinking if I did not get up they would go to sleep and not work for me. I slowly uncrossed my legs, got up, and sat on the couch. This took me all afternoon to, as I say, "Pull my act together." I had class that night with Corine and had to get a ride there, no way was I driving. As soon as I got there, she asked me what had happened to me as I was glowing and my aura was out about four feet. For two weeks, I could answer just about any question anyone had. Of course, they were not ready for the answers so just as quickly forgot them, but it was great knowing the answers till I began telling someone something they were not ready for. Then somehow I knocked a Coke over on me and irritated lost my train of thought. I have always felt it was my spirit telling me to shut up. A skeptical friend asked me to read the Tarot cards for him one day and I told him he should not ask unless he really wanted to know because I would tell him the truth. He said, "Yeah, yeah, go ahead." I did. It was not a good reading and he thought I was just making it up. He left mad. About two weeks later, what I had said happened verbatim and he came over, apologized to me, and said he would never call the Tarot crazy again. I explained to him again that all I had done was interpret what his spirit knows and had answered through the cards. The Tarot cards are not that difficult to master. It takes time to memorize the meanings but most people use the books available which shows all the different meanings for the cards. When you shuffle the cards you have to focus "only" on what you want to know about. If you do not do this, then all the other garbage from the day bleeds into the reading. Pick a layout and stick with it until you learn it . When you begin to read the cards, the meanings vary within the same card, but you will find that the one meant for you will stand out to you. You are getting in touch with your spirit, your angel. The same one that pats you on the back when you are distraught or full of tears.

One evening I was standing over the wall heater talking to my husband about what I experienced when I was suddenly in the middle of a vision. I knew I was still in my living room, but in front ofme was rolling golden hills and one huge oak tree. Next to it on the right side, was one of those little Chinese bridges that seemed to go from the hill the tree was on to another hill, but that was it, no water under it. There was nothing else to it and as I stared trying to take in all I could and figure out what I was being shown, my husband reached out and touched my arm and said my name with worry in his voice. I was immediately pulled back from where ever I was and looked at him, who now sat there with fear in his eyes. All he knew was one moment I had been talking to him and the next had seemed to be gone though my body was still standing there leaning against the wall. I believe what that vision meant is that I had created a bridge to the physical world, because the bridge was on my right. I am the Oak Tree. By letting my energy go up and then down, I had reached the heights and was then able to convey it to others in a manner better understood by them..

A few days later I made Chili Verde Pork burritos. The voice of my spirit came to me again and said that unless I stopped smoking and eating meat or doing anything that harmed the temple, my body, it would have to go back down, as it could not be party to this. I asked if I could have children like this and heard, "No". I knew I had promised to bring two souls into this life, and I was not ready to give up Chili Verde Pork burritos or smoking. I asked if l could come back to this state later. It said "Yes, but it will be more difficult". I said, "But I can do it?" I heard "Yes". Therefore, I decided to wait for a while, as I knew I was supposed to bring two souls into the world.

My husband began acting as if I was crazy because I knew things, and because he was afraid of what I knew. I told him his brother would come looking for his mother and within two weeks, he did. He had never met his brother as his father had left his mother before he knew she was pregnant again, and had taken their first son with him. So neither boy knew they had a brother. He could not deal with it and it scared him that I was right. He was happy to get drunk with his friends and party and it did not seem to me that he wanted to do anything with his life. I wanted to do something with my life and we grew apart. I meditated and asked my guides why this was happening, and was shown a vision. I saw myself only I had dark black hair and I was standing in reeds by the water.

My husband was with me and he was afraid because guards were going to catch us, so he was going to run away and leave me there. I was from some temple and the guards would kill me if they found me with him. He left me there, I died because of it, and it created Karma between us. I understood from the scene what happened. I also knew that I had to break up with him in this life, do so, and remain friends so that the Karma stopped, we would not have more Karma to deal with in the future. I also knew there was no way he would understand this. We broke up and it took many months. He was so distraught and could not see we had grown apart and I could not go back to the way I was. He was happy to sit around and talk about people or watch shows that were so negative to me I just could not deal with it. I could not go back to what I had been before. Once you learn something, you can not just forget about it. Finally, I left. The day I was moving out he tackled me on the stairs out the back door, trying to make me change my mind and hurt my back. I moved to El Cerrito with two other friends and then found another friend who needed a room mate.

Chapter Six

Shortly after leaving my husband, I went to a Gypsy fortune teller that my father had gone to who had told him many things. So I figured she *was* talented and this would be a good test for her. She read my palm and because I knew where everything *was* in my astrology chart, she could tell me a lot. She told me that by the time I died, I would have everything I ever wanted. I looked at her like she *was* trying to con me and said, "Come on, don't say this if it isn't true." "I want a lot of things that are not ordinary, like enlightenment, and developing telepathy and my kinetic abilities besides for millions of dollars." She repeated herself and said by the time you die you will have everything you have ever wanted. So far I have except for the million dollars, so I think she *was* right.

My sister *was* taking me to the movies for my 23rd birthday in Berkeley and had to park down the street from the theater. As we walked up the street, we passed a shop where they were having meditation classes. Something stopped me at the door and I stood there looking in for a moment. A man came to the door and asked us ifwe wanted to join them. My sister spoke to him, *as* I stood there unable to speak. Finally I thought, "he's a stoned fox", and he looked at me *as* if I had just said it aloud. I blushed. He looked at me and asked me if I wanted to stay for the meeting. I did but I could not disappoint my sister so said, ''No, we are going to the movie for my birthday." The Wind and the Lion *was* playing. He thought that *was* a good movie and told us to have a good time. He said he would be there for a few days if I were interested in learning about it and we left. He would be my third teacher but I did not know it yet, and I do not believe he remembered me at this point from Ravenna Park. I did not go back until it *was* too late. The energy between us *was* just plain overwhelming and I could not bring myself to go down there until later and it was too late, they had left town and gone back east. He was the Wind (Aquarius) and I was the Lion(Leo). Remember there is no such thing as coincidence ...

Life moved on and I had moved to Albany, left the fabric store, and started working at a bank. One night we had a strip party for one of the girls who was to be married. We rented a club and the stripper was late. This was all the rage in the 70's and many guys worked their way through college stripping. Finally, the guy shows up and puts on some really unusual music that sounded almost East Indian. Then he started dancing. He was weaving a spell and I was the only one there who knew it. I wrapped myself and pushed my aura out and he danced faster. He seemed to notice I had wrapped and came over in front of me to dance. He stayed there much to my chagrin, until I finally thought, "It isn't my wedding you are dancing in front of the wrong woman." He then moved over to dance in front of the girl who was to be married. The girl next to me asked me, "What was he doing?" I just shook my head and visibly exhaled... There was absolutely no way she would understand what just happened. He was Tantric dancing, the only male I have ever seen do it. When he stopped dancing they put on regular music and we all started dancing. He came and asked me to dance. After dancing, he told me he was not a stripper anymore and had not done it in a long time, and then only to make tuition for college. He taught classes in philosophy and meditation and would I like to drop my life and fly to the east coast and be his student? Yes, he was serious. I could not leave my cats. They were the only things that stopped me from going. It was the same person I had met in Ravenna Park so long ago and again on San Pablo Avenue in Berkeley. I did not out of a sense of responsibility, though I wished at the time I had the nerve to just pick up, leave, and start over again.

They say when the student is ready the teacher will appear, and he had, once when I was too young to follow him, though I would have in a heartbeat; then again, when I had finally become free again with my whole life in front of me. Only I had pets and a job and I have always taken it very seriously that humanity was here to help take care of the animals not use and abuse them.

The apartment I shared with my girlfriend had a huge sofa and two of her boyfriends had cut the back legs off so it sat at a tilt like a cock pit. One evening I sat down to meditate and sunk deep into samadi. I woke around three in the morning after what felt like me falling into my body. I was still sitting up in a meditation posture with my hands on my knees palms up and was almost stiff I had been sitting like that was for so long. I sat there for a moment because it felt like someone was in the room with me, it was very eerie, but it dissipated after a few minutes. I had sat down about 7 p.m. and could not believe I had just meditated for 8 hours nonstop. I was wide awake after that and decided to get up and get ready for work. One thing deep meditation does do for you is give you energy so when you first learn how to do it, it is better done in the morning especially at about three A. M.

My life took an interesting turn then. I met some new friends. One was a girl who had run away from home at a very young age and ended up in some kind of satanic cult. Her husband found her when she had run away from them and took her in. I took this with a grain of salt because I did not really believe in Satan. For me, to believe in Satan gave him power. It was not long before I was trying to heal, read Tarot, and generally trying to help others with the new abilities, I had discovered. I figured what were they for if not to use, much to the chagrin of Prometheus who was constantly trying to get me to tone it down. I had one friend Greg, who had developed cancer of the intestines. He was about 23 when this happened. One day he stopped by my place on the way to a party in San Francisco and I tried to heal him. After a couple of minutes I heard my guide say, "Stop now or it will flow back into you. You can not do anything more for him now." So I stopped. He felt great, he said. He left and went on to his party. The next day he called and told me he had felt like he used to feel when he was healthy before the cancer. He had over done it at the party though and felt awful then. I told him I could not do it anymore or I would pick it up like back wash. He understood. He died about six months later. I had told him about two months prior to that about the deal that my two best friends and I had made with each other. That if one of us died, no matter when it was, that they would come back and tell the other two that there was an after life. The night he died he came to me in a dream and told me he really loved me and wished we had had more time together. Then I woke up. It was so real, I called even though it was early in the morning. His father answered and talked to me for a while. He had died in the early hours of the night and he had not been to sleep yet. He was surprised that I called so quickly, and I told him about my dream. He said he had mentioned me often to him and he really cared a lot about our friendship. It was a sad start to the day. I learned early on that many times you can not tell people what you see about them.

Either they do not see it and their ego gets very upset at you because it is just not ready to acknowledge that the soul and spirit are really in control, or they do understand but their family does not and the Hordes of Aries come at you that way.

The classes I had taken had helped me to develop other talents too. Finding things for people became a fun past time. Whenever my friends lost something, they would ask me and many times, we found whatever it was they had misplaced within minutes. Some people thought it was great that I could do this and others were frightened by it. To me this is nothing, nowhere near, what I want to be able to do, and yet people were genuinely freaked out about it. It is strange, the prejudices we run into from our friends or the ones we work with because we have talents they have not bothered to try to develop. I have always told people that anyone could do what I do they would just have to practice. Everyone has a natural ability and with practice, it comes out. Some people are better at telepathy and some will be better at healing or psychometry or some other ability. It is just like breaking a leg and being laid up in bed for a while, you have to learn how to walk all over again and use those muscles. Psychic development is the same way. My first teacher Corine would say, "They have not used those muscles in a long time and they have to learn how to use them all over again." People lack patience though; they would try a few times and if It did not work, would give up. One day Patty's husband showed up at my door saying he did not know who else to turn to. Patty, he felt was possessed. I literally rolled my eyes at him. He then said she is speaking in a weird voice that is not hers and sounds like a guy. I said, "Oh come on, I don't even know if l believe in possession." "Please come look at her would you?" he begged. I did. Half way out of curiosity if a person really could be possessed, but not really thinking it would be anything. He went on ahead of me and I drove my own car over. One of the things I had learned in my first psychic development class was to wrap myself in white light if I felt I was in danger. Another was to consult my guide. On the way over, I did this. All he said was, "You don't fight hate with hate?" I answered, ''No," but was at a loss as to what to do anyway. When I got there, Patty was setting on a beanbag chair and she seemed out of it. I asked her husband if she was on anything, but he was unaware of anything. Then she looked up and said in a deep husky voice, "What is she doing here?" I looked at her unable to believe my friend had just said this about me and said her name. "Patty, are you ok?" That same deep voice came out of her and when she looked at me it was pure malevolence. Ok something was going on and I still did not know what I was going to do about it, or if I could do anything about it. I looked at her husband and said, "Well I don't know if I can help but I will wrap her and see if that helps." I sat across the room from her. I called her name again and she looked at me. I began pulling energy in from the ether and sending white light to her. Her husband and a friend of his were sitting against the other wall to my right. She said something about us having a staring contest and began staring back at me. I continued to send white light to her and after a moment, I realized what I needed to do and began sending her love. Complete compassion and love within pure white light. I began to see a white light an inch or so in front of me as though it were coming out of my third eye and stretching across the room. At the same time, I could see dark dirty looking energy coming out of her stretching towards me across the room. When the light energy touched in the middle of the room, I just kind of pushed mentally and the white light began taking over the dark and pushing it back towards Patty. When it had made its way to her and was beginning to touch her, for a split second I saw a look of pure hatred and then she was absorbed in it and glowing and smiling. I wanted to make sure what ever was in her was out and I jerked my head slightly. When I did this, she flew off the beanbag chair and into the wall behind her, not hard but enough to shake her up and wake her up. When I looked over at her husband and his friend, they both had their mouths hanging open and were not moving. I laughed at the look on their faces and her husband jumped up and said, "What just happened there?" "What did you do?" "How did you do that?" I asked him if he saw the light. He said, "light?" I said, "Yeah, white light," and asked his friend also. All they could say was that they saw something in the air between us but were not sure what it was. Patty came to, wide-awake, and back to her normal self. I left after that as it was late and I had to work the next day.

A short time later Patty came over and told me about a teacher who was teaching manifestation. He was giving classes at a place close by in Oakland. I learned a main stay for my life from this teacher. He had a PHD in language and according to him; the mind understood words differently than we did. For instance in math a positive and a negative cancel each other out. Well how many times do you use positives and negatives in the same sentence in a day? We learn these laws of math or language but rarely see how they work in our lives. He explained that words like can't or isn't are really a positive and a negative combined and when the mind hears them it automatically cancelled them out so sentences like, "I can't stand it when you smoke," would be heard by the mind as, "I stand it when you smoke." To make matters worse, the person you were talking to, well their mind would do the same thing, and so they would keep smoking around you. When asked why they did, they would usually say, "I don't know." They did know too. The spirit of a person does not care whether you say it or you hear it from someone else. If you accept it and do not negate it, then your spirit thinks this is acceptable to you and sets out to give it to you. He taught us that if you focus your attention on accidents that they would come to you in some way. That was one reason there were so many accidents.

For instance sometimes you may see an accident and at the same time think the car looks like someone you know. In this case your spirit sees you focusing on your friend having an accident an sends that energy wave out. Now if your friend is above this and does not accept the energy coming in they are fine and it does not happen to them, or they may have a close call. Between what we watch on T.V., the movies, or the "Looky Lou's" starring at accidents, it is a wonder we can make it down the road in one piece. He taught us to say, "Not for me" when we caught ourselves looking at, or focusing on anything we did not want coming into our life. It may be bad English but if you say, "It's not for me," then the mind cancels out the "is" and the "not" as a positive and a negative, so what it really hears is, "It for me". Is this what we wanted? No. We also learned that when you do this for three days, the first thing you notice is it gets worse. The reason is that when you start saying, "Not for me," you are stopping the negative wave that you do not want in your life anymore, but the stuff you allowed in prior to this has to run it's course.

Therefore, things speed up and it seems like it is getting worse and so, many will think this does not work, and stop trying. If you do this for a week or two, and consciously catch yourself, you begin to see where all the things happening to you are coming from. This is because it does speed up and once you are through that lull period where the old negativity that you had already set up is finished then all the thoughts you are allowing begin coming to you. Then you learn who is creating your life, and that it is "you" and your thoughts that are setting you up. Then if you keep it up, the negative things begin to fade because you are catching yourself and your focus is only on the things you want. Just like Thoth and many other masters have said, "Focus only on the light." This phrase does not mean that negative things do not happen, it means they do happen to those that focus on them or allow others in their life to focus on them. This is you the soul, consciously controlling your thoughts and not letting your brain(ego) to automatically take over the drivers seat. It is amazing what happens when you really focus on doing this. Your life begins to flow with your thoughts and things seem to happen overnight. It takes a lot of focus though mostly due to what others think you should have in your life. One thing it does do is make you more aware of what others are doing that is affecting your life. Like commercials that you suck into, or movies that you become absorbed by that literally steal your imagination from you for a time. Your spirit is creating this world for you, based on your thoughts, and your imagination. If you focus on something your spirit thinks you want it in your life and sets out to gi e it to you. Make you think about all those computer games full of war? Majority wins in this joint universe we inhabit together. So when enough people are playing or watching another person play a war game, what is that telling all their spirits? Or TV shows about space wars. You want that in your life? Where is their focus? Your attention has been stolen then, take it back.

Worrying is one of the worst things you can do because your focus is totally on what ever you are worried about. Your spirit thinks you want it otherwise you would not put all your attention and energy on it, right? It does not question why you want it, it knows you will learn not to fear it and that you will be able to handle it and live through it, and that is one of your spirits main jobs. To help the soul learn and evolve and become what the spirit thinks is equal with it. The spirit and soul are also leaning how to work with each other and understand each other. It may seem like this is automatic but it is not. The spirit is intellectual, telepathic and the soul is empathic and emotional. The soul imagines everything and the spirit takes what the soul imagines and creates it with thought waves. The ego has figured this out and steals the imagination of the soul to create what it wants with it.

Another great friend I met at the same time was Jonathan. One day I took him to one of the classes in psychic development. Most of these classes were a majority of women and so his bubbly energy from all the attention was just too much for them. Right before the end of class one of the women decided, he as a male was draining them of energy. What can I say; people get strange ideas about people they know very little about. Also their focus was on how men drain women of energy so by focusing on this they gave it energy and poor Jonathan was being bombarded with all this energy and was almost bouncing off the walls. Someone mentioned it to me, and I of course stood up for him but decided it was time for us to go anyway. It took about forty-five minutes to get home from there and it was a dark stretch of highway to get there. As I drove, I began to get this intense thought to pull over. It was a highway though and the thought made no sense to me at all, so I tried to ignore it. It became stronger to the point that it was disrupting my ability to concentrate and I began to feel energy pouring into my head from behind like I was being psychically attacked. Jonathan knew something was up by the look on my face and finally said, "Are you ok?" I could not focus on driving and answer him as the energy would have me pulling over, but Jonathan wanted an answer. I was driving an Alpha Romeo Spider Veloce at the time and Jonathan was six foot tall. I finally yelled, "No, I will not pull over, Jonathan is my friend and will not hurt me and was not trying to hurt them," at which Jonathan looked over at me as a streetlight flashed behind me and saw a Gray alien sitting right behind me. The energy dissipated from me after I said that. I did not know he was right behind me and Jonathan had just seen him, but suddenly Jonathan was trying to cram himself into the cubbyhole where his feet go, backside first, which is a pretty small area. This was so funny looking to me, I stopped frowning and started laughing and asked, "What are you doing?" The whole time he had not taken his eyes off the space behind me. The being faded away and Jonathan craned his head to make sure he was gone and twisted back up and back in his seat. All he would say for a half an hour was, "Whoa." When I pulled up to his house, he frantically looked at me and said, "Are you going to be ok?" He was tom between his fear and my safety; when all he wanted to do was, get the hell out of the car. He still had not mentioned what he saw behind me so I thought he meant my outburst and I apologized and explained that I felt like I was fighting not to pull over and that I would have to talk to the teacher about this as I felt like I was being attacked. It was not until the next day that he finally told me what he saw behind me. Prometheus had been alerted by others that I might be in danger and so had taken appropriate measures. Once I had my outburst he had gotten the whole picture from me and further reading Jonathan had agreed with my assessment and left.

Jonathan and I had many exploits together. One day he showed up at my house and was all excited. When I got him to calm down, he told me he had gone to a meditation meeting and the person there was powerful energy wise.

When you walked into the room the energy was vibrating. At the end of the meeting, he walked up and talked to the teacher. For some reason he showed the teacher a picture of me and the teacher had asked him if I knew what I was? I looked at Jonathan and said, "What did he mean by that?" Jonathan did not know. Many times over the next ten years or so, I would hear or be asked that same question, and none of them would ever tell me what they meant by that.

Another time he came over upset because a friend had promised him a ride to San Francisco to a meeting where they were recruiting people into a group and did not show. As it was a spiritual group, I was then talked into driving over. When we walked in, the minute I entered the room I felt a draining sort of energy and wrapped Jonathan and myself. The main person came and spoke to us and I asked him what his group was all about. He said that one day a ship would come and pick them up and they would leave and go off to other worlds. This was great I thought but as we spoke to him there was one thing I could not seem to fathom and this man was very vague about. That was how they were going to get on the ship. I asked if the ship would land and he said no. Then

I read his mind, I saw his answer plain as daylight. What was worse, he also saw that I saw it. I said, "You know that isn't the way, that is running from what you are suppose to do down here." He said, "How would you know what I was suppose to do?" I told him that giving up his life that was a gift to him, is not the answer and he would have to come back and do it all over again if he did. He glanced around to see if anyone had heard me and got a scared look on his face. He then called his bodyguard students over and told them to throw us out. They walked up to us and I took one look at them and said, "Don't touch me, I'm leaving." I looked at him once more and said, "You know I am right." He said, "You are stuck and don't see the truth, this is a prison." Many years later the same group, were found dead in LA. I am sure many of you might be thinking why did not you stop them? Well what could I say, "I read his mind?" What could I prove? It is difficult for those in the west who have had their energy rise because of our society. Sometimes they do not listen to their spirit as I had, and loose their mind(spirit) to chaos, or are stuck in a mental ward because they see things differently than others or that others can not see. Sometimes they end up on drugs that mess with the flow of energy and their spirit steps

back from them. Society does not understand how they

can read their minds and know how they feel because they

are controlled by their egos. . When you walk by someone

who has had their energy rise and think how stupidly they

are dressed, they hear it, and unless they have learned a

great deal of compassion for your egotistically critical and

insensitive attitude they are likely to say something to you.

Only once you have experienced the oneness it is a very

difficult thing to forever remember it and not be there. It

brings great sadness and takes a very strong will to look to

the future and know you will be there again. Please note

I said strong will, not ego. It feels like missing the boat a

hundred times over. Being around people who's thoughts

and feelings you hear and feel is down right painful. I

became very empathic whether from this or my time with

Prometheus I am not sure. You eventually learn to block

or ignore others so you can return to a somewhat regular

life, but you can never forget where you were and so you

strive to get back there consciously. I came to see that while

in that state there are so many people who just can not

comprehend you, that it is like a genius talking to a child. I then felt like maybe this was a chance for me to walk a fence and be able to explain to others as a sort of middle ground, and that is what I have tried to do.

There was another time I went to San Francisco with Jonathan for another group. You would think I would have learned form the first group, but I did not know what I was suppose to be doing either. I felt that at least Jonathan would not be getting into any weird cults with me around. So once again, we went to a meeting. There were many people in the room and it seemed positive enough so, we went in. Five or six people came up to us from different directions and offered us a drink or a cookie. They started asking us questions about our selves and I answered them truthfully. One said I think my mentor will want to speak to you. He went and got another person and he came over and started pumping me with questions. It was such a switch I looked at Jonathan and then back at the man and asked him what his problem was. He was attacking me verbally and seemed to think I had an alien in me and it was his duty to get it out. I laughed. I could not help it. Then the circle started to close and one of them put their hand on my arm. I jerked my arm away and said, "Don't touch me." This idiot seemed bent on attaching himself to my arm and trying to hold me there, while the person bereted me as if I were going to run. I looked this other person in the eye and said, "If you don't get your hand off me right now you will regret it." Jonathan was standing there with his mouth open, as he could not believe what he was witnessing. They acted as if they were the best of my friends and tried to con me but it was too late. I looked at Jonathan and said, "I'm out of here, and if you want a ride you better follow me NOW." One thing about Jonathan, I never had to spell out anything for him. With few words, he would follow my lead. They actually tried to stop us at the door and I told him if he did not get his hand off me, I would scream for the police. He pointed around him and said I have many people here who would say you came in and started trouble. That is when I pushed my aura out. A few backed up but the main person did not and was still standing in my way. I looked him in the eye and said ok if you want to play games, just remember you started this and began sending white light energy into him. He put his hand up and said, "We don't want her, she's evil." I looked at him and said, "And you are a sick control freak." I walked past him a few steps and then after all that, he said, "You better not bad mouth us to anyone." That was the last seminar I ever went to with Jonathan. I was so angry on the way home he did not say much but," How was I suppose to know they would be like that?" Indeed how would anyone, I thought. Anyone who tries to brainwash you or force you to believe like them, "For your own good", has a control problem, I said. I hated to think what would have happened to Jonathan at both of those meetings without me. It was down right scary to think about it. People have to learn at their own speed, and I believe that your spirit will make sure something like that happens if it is not right for you.

Chapter Seven

A few years later, I became pregnant, I had my son. I knew my first would be a boy from an earlier dream I had years before and I knew the moment I became pregnant. Shortly after he was born I had a dream about my Grand mother on my fathers side. She was just checking up on me and told me I should call my aunt. I did and found out she had died the night before at the hospital. She had been upset at not seeing me in so long and she got to see her grandson on the astral before she went on her way. I worked for a while at a bank but was now a mother and tried to be a responsible parent. Sherman's father still wanted to party, and I could not. I broke up with him and I moved back to Seattle to stay with my parents and begin over. Once back home, nothing was the same. All my old friends from high school were gone and had moved away. I found a job and went about trying to make a life for my son and I. I worked in downtown Seattle and one day was giving a fellow worker a ride. We walked down the street and waited at the light to walk across to the parking lot. There was a Native American man and a girl on the comer across from us and when the light changed we met in the middle of the street. My friend, a Scorpio, and I were talking and she looked up at them as we walked by and thought something derogatory and the girl swung at her slapping her as hard as she could. I immediately grabbed my friend and yelled at them and the man had grabbed the girl and apologized saying she had been through a ceremony or something and was not herself. My friend now with a hand mark on her face said, "That's ok, it was my fault." We walked off and I asked her what she was talking about. She told me she had thought how dirty the girl looked, like she had slept in her clothes, and the girl had looked at her like she read her *mind* and slapped her. So I had to wonder at this point if people began reading others minds if it would cause more problems instead of fixing them. I am sure though that my Scorpio friend did not make that mistake again, and learned to guard her thoughts closer.

At first while I was saving money, I stayed with my mother and step-father. They felt they had done their stint as parents and did not want to baby sit all the time. With my son, it was too much for them and I moved in with another friend and rented a room in her home. She had two older kids and they enjoyed talking to me. My son was about three at the time. I had just come outside with him and Ben, her son. I was talking to Ben and Sherman was running around on the grass. I heard a car coming down the street racing fast and started walking towards Sherman. The closer I got to him, the closer he would run towards the street thinking it was a game. Finally Ben noticed what was going on and said, "Here let me try." Sherman was only two feet from the curb and I was afraid he would run right in front of the car so I said, "No wait," and reached out to grab his arm. Sherman saw this and started running as if it were a game. At that moment, the car, a Taxi, is flying by and Sherman runs into the street. The woman driving, seeing him, hits her brakes, and I scream "NO" and reach out with my hand in their direction. In a split second, I knew that if Sherman was not scared bad he would go into the street again. As I reached at the car with my hand,

I felt like I had control of it. I saw it screech to a halt right in front of him not hitting him, and then tail end swing over, I jerked my fingers, and it barely nudges him and makes him sit down. As I saw this, I was moving my hand as if I had hold of the car. Then it was over. Ben standing next to me had taken all this in, turned to look at me and said, "How did you do that?" He had seen the whole thing standing next to me, had seen me reach, and the car moving for me as I moved my hand. In the mean time I ran down and in one arm had Sherman and in the other the female Taxi driver who was in shock. I told her to slow down now and remember speeding was not meant for residential areas. I asked Ben not to tell his friends because if it got out they would tum me into a guinea pig, and he understood this. Sherman was fine, just scared, and he never went into the street again. I felt drained for the rest of the day from the shock of it all. I never thought about these things when they happened, they just happened and I reacted quickly enough to do something.

A few months later, I moved into a one-bedroom apartment in Fremont with French window's and a seat in the living room. I used the living room for my bedroom and let my son have the room. I was working forty hours at my job and going to computer classes in the evenings. I could not afford a baby sitter and so my mother would watch Sherman. The one time I went out with a friend after class for an hour my stepfather had a fit. They did not want to baby sit and felt they had done their job as parents. I felt like my life had taken a tum for the worse and so started to meditate again looking for an answer to what I should be doing in life. I felt that if l was doing what my soul wanted me to do, life would be flowing better. In meditation I was free to do what I wanted to do so I worked on my universe in the astral, building my place up the way I wanted it with trees and planets. I talked to my guide; Prometheus up there and finally asked him if l would ever have another physical teacher. I would also talk to him telepathically but at this point in time I was not fully aware of the many times I spoke with him. Now looking back, I realize I was talking to him but at the time I simply thought they were my thoughts or my inner selfs thoughts.

One night about a week after my conversation with him about a physical teacher, I had a lucid dream that my younger sister and I had to go to her work place and pick up some posters. We arrived at her business and inside the building, there were swinging doors with windows in the top portion. (Very much like the doors I blew the little blue aliens back through the first time I was taken). Suddenly she said, "Did you hear that?" A noise and a shadow through the window of the door had frightened her. No one was supposed to be there as it was the weekend. If you have ever had a dream were something menacing comes around a corner and you know it's going to come around the corner, well this was one of those dreams only I was "conscious" in it and was determined not to let it turn into a nightmare. I said, "Come on let's get out of here," not willing to play this game. All the way to the car, I felt someone following us only when we turned around a door would swing or a shadow through a window was all we would see. We finally got to her car, slammed the doors, and took off. Suddenly I see a streak come across the parking lot as we are leaving. I tell my sister to hurry and she sped up. Suddenly a person jumps onto the side of her car with a thud, and is holding on to the door as we are driving down the street. I am determined not to get scared as I felt like if I did then it would be like being on the defensive and I might as well give up. My sister says, "What was that?" She is not looking over, as she is driving. I said, "There is a guy hanging off the side of your car." I have always found it amazing that in lucid dreams the people that are props that you make up act exactly as if the person would in real life. Here my sister, a prop, inhaled just as she would have and said, "Ah, What is he doing?" I looked at her and said, "I don't know", and looked over at him, "He's staring at me." It was a game and I was becoming bored with it and not willing to allow them to turn this into a nightmare. "What does he want?" she asked me. So I asked him, "What do you want?' He just stared at me. I stared back at him for a while, and asked again, what he wanted. He still did not answer me, so I opened the door and knocked him off. Meantime my sister is freaking out because he is now chasing us. I tell her to drop me off at my house and go get help and he will come after me so she will be ok. She does and I run into this house I do not know but is suppose to be where I am living and start locking doors. I yell to see if my son is there and there is no answer. I pick up the phone and it will not work. I run to the back door, they were double doors to a deck, and he was coming up the steps to the deck.

I run through the kitchen and into a hall and am hiding. I am trying to be as quiet as possible but I can hear my heart pounding and my own breathing so loudly that I am sure he will find me. I look around for something to protect myself with and all I can find is a flashlight. There is a swinging door to the kitchen, he starts backing through it, and I hit him it the head, and the whole dream exploded as Kundalini rose in me for the second time in this life. I woke and flew up off the bed and froze there in the quiet. It was so real, I was still vibrating from the energy, and now suddenly back in my room and I listened for any sound in my room. I felt a presence and wrapped the blankets around me, shaking. I wrapped myself, called to my guide, and sat there looking out my window for hours telepathically talking to him. I looked up at one point and saw a star shooting to the left. Finally, I was so exhausted I passed out. For the next two weeks, I could not get the dream out of my mind. One day Bea, a girlfriend, came over and suggested that I draw his picture. She found that when she did this with dreams and other things that she could not get out of her head it helped. I tried and with her help, I drew a pretty good likeness of the person. After that,

I was ok. A few weeks later my sons father called and said he was getting married and wanted Sherman and I to come down to the Bay Area for the wedding. I went and stayed with a girlfriend in Point Richmond. There was a huge deck around her apartment and after my son was picked up by his dad to go out for a while, I went and laid in the sun. I vividly to this day remember creating this beautiful golden land with a forest in the dream and meeting a beautiful golden haired male on the astral plane and doing more than talking to him. Then suddenly another man that lived next door and shared the deck was standing four feet from me saying, "Wake up", "Hello", "Can you hear me?" I stirred from a very deep sleep to see this strange man who was worried I would start screaming and was apologizing for waking me but I was turning very red and he thought I should go inside. I was red too. I had forgotten how hot the sun was when I drifted off. So a few days later, I went to the wedding red on the front and white on the back. First though I went to see my cousins while I was there to get my hair done. While sitting in her chair, she received a phone call and stopped to answer it. I was looking around her office and saw a book on the table. I picked it up and there is the person from my dream. "I don't believe it", I

exclaimed, "Who is this?" I demanded, not sure whether to be

upset or not. It seemed so planned and I stared at my cousin.

My cousin looked at her sister and said that is a friend of mine

who teaches philosophy classes. I told her about the dream

and bought the book from her to bring back and show to Bea.

About a month later, I would transfer with my job to LA and

move with my son down there to take classes from him. In the

east if a man leaves his family to pursue spiritual pursuits no

one thinks bad of him, yet here in the west if a woman moves

like I did even though I did not leave my son, I was thought

strange. This was and is my calling. I have always been

happier talking and investigating the unknown than anything

I have done otherwise. The puzzling thing for me in all of this

was why I did not seem able to control my abilities and use

them for what I wanted. They always seemed to be there for

me when I needed them yet if I tried to prove to someone that

I could do something it was not dependable enough. I found

this infuriating yet reasoned that the ability was not meant

for egotistical applications. I applied for and was accepted

to classes in philosophy and psychic development in Los

Angeles. The teacher well versed in Eastern philosophy as well as being enlightened. I can hear the questions that last sentence called into your mind even as I am writing this. Not only was he the man in my dream, but also I went on to speak to him telepathically before I even left the Northwest. Before I received the letter telling me I was accepted to the classes, he had already informed me the night before in my dreams. A week before I left I had a job I could transfer to in Los Angeles so I would not have to find work too. It was all rather magical, and I loved it. I have always gotten the biggest kick out of magic, see that is where my love and focus are, so I guess that explains why all this stuff happens to me.

I set up a moving company to move my things down and would call me at my new job two weeks later. This meant I had to drive down, find a place to live and a day care for my son in two weeks. I stopped off in the Bay Area to see my cousins and one decided to come with me and the other kept my son and would meet us in two weeks. That gave me a little more time to get myself established and find a place to live. On the drive to Los Angeles, we stopped in Oxnard for lunch and walked across railroad tracks to sit on the grass and stare at the water. As we sat down and began eating, two dolphins began jumping out of the water putting on a show for us. We drove around in Los Angeles all day and finally found a motel we could afford and slept. The next few days we found a place to live. The property owner a woman, lived in front of me and I rented a cottage in the backyard. It had a bougainvillea arbor outside that was beautiful, and down the drive was passion fruit vine. I had a garden out front in November. I was amazed. After we knew each other a little better, she asked me if I was Aryan. At the time, the only Aryan race I knew of was the one that Hitler had spoken of during World War II. She told me that the real Aryans used to live above Pakistan in the mountains and they were of a fair complexion with red or black hair and green eyes or rust colored eyes. Years later my mother would tell me that her mothers father who they thought had been English, because he had changed his name to Jones, had really come from Armenia an area above India and Pakistan.

Classes did not begin for another week, so I had time to settle into my new habitat. The first day of classes, I dressed all in lapis blue with lapis jewelry. My hair was cut in a long

Cleopatra style and then I had it permed for ease in the heat.

There were about 400 students there, waiting for our teacher

to come in. They had rented a hall because there were so many

students. I stood talking to my cousins who knew him. I, at

the time had not realized he was the same man who ran into

the wedding in the park, or whom I had met on the San Pablo

Avenue in Berkeley with my sister. For me I had only spoken

to him telepathically or so I thought. That in the beginning

tends to make you feel like you are fantasizing and makes it

hard to believe when the person is not in front of you. As I

stood there waiting and talking, suddenly I felt the energy

change. I looked at my cousin and said, "What was that?" She

smiled and said, "Oh is he here then?" and looked around.

She grabbed my shoulders, said, " wait now," and would not

let me turn around as if it were some big surprise. Then she

backed away. I turned around, and the others had cleared

a path between us, and about fifteen feet in front of me he

stood. I smiled at him and thought he had gained weight

since the cover on his book. He frowned ever so slightly and I

realized he could read my mind and blushed. I had not meant

that he looked bad, only that he had gained weight since the cover of the book and thought as much. The energy was so intense that I finally opened my arms and gave it back to him. I was grinning ear to ear and could not stop. Being around an enlightened being tends to do this and makes you feel silly because you have a grin that you cannot get rid of. I had around twenty people watching my reaction.

After that day, I could tell when he walked into the room. The energy perceptibly changed and would almost buzz it vibrated so and anyone who was his student would start smiling. During another class, Rama came up to me afterwards and we spoke a while. I asked him what he had meant when he asked Jonathan if l knew what I was. He stopped me and asked, "Who is Jonathan?" I explained that Jonathan had attended a meeting in Berkeley with someone he had described that I thought was him. This person had asked Jonathan if I knew what I was. He asked me what my name was, and I looked at him strangely knowing he knew my name and asked him, "What do you mean?" He said, "How do you say it, how do "you" pronounce it?" So, I said it for him. He made me say it over and over slowly as I say it differently sometimes. Jah nit, Jah nuit, and Jah net. After hearing this, he asked me if l had ever studied Kabalism. I had not and he suggested I buy a book and read up on it, he said there were a few Goddesses with names like mine but he could not remember exactly what they meant. Even so, it would be another ten years before I bought my first book on Kabalism and found out what he meant that day.

I took two quarters of classes with him and then he moved to the east coast. I could not afford to move again and could not drag my son all over. I did not think that would be fair to him so I stayed in LA. I was very upset that I could not go and I have no doubt that Rama felt it. He would frequently speak to all of his students in dreams and teach them on the Astral plane. The night of June 18, 1985 I dreamed of an old girlfriend who had run off with a guy and left me with a large phone bill. We went to a strange city to find someone and then she turned into another friend and left with yet another one and left me there in this strange city. I had a car and I went to a phone booth and called Rama to let him know I was coming to the class. I dialed the number 990-1242 or 51 (not really his number) and I heard a recording come on. It was Rama and he said, "He who follows others is surely lost, but he who forges his own path shall surely succeed." This was his way of telling me that I was not meant to go East with them and I needed to forge my own path. If you notice the number is all 9's and the 1242 and 1251 total nine and are 9 apart. In Astrology the ninth house is the house of higher learning and Sagittarius ruled by Jupiter.

Chapter Eight

With all of my spiritual support seemingly gone except for Prometheus, I decided to settle into work and see if I could make progress in that part of my life. At the time I was doing inventory for 7 restaurants and an accounts receivable spread sheet with the inventory included. Our offices were three floors below ground, and I was standing in front of my desk talking to the woman at the next desk when I suddenly felt a wave of energy that made me sit down. I told the other woman, something just happened and it did not feel good. My first thoughts were for my son, or family. I felt like many people had just died, it was the only way I could describe it.

Like I had just felt them all scream at once and pass right through me. I left and went home to check on my son and he was alright. I took him home and called my mother and she was alright. Then I turned on the news and saw where a construction company that was building a high rise downtown about 5 blocks from us had put too many steel beams on the fifth floor up and it had collapsed and killed all the guys on the floors beneath them. It was a terrible accident and many men died. That is what I felt.

It was a short time later I met my daughters' father. Although he had a lot of potential, he seemed to feel the world owed him and because of it did not get as far as he felt he deserved.

I had a chance to transfer to Denver with my work and I thought it might help him get away from the area and start fresh. I was still young and naive. I had always tried to change myself for the better and thought anyone could do it. I sent my son up to my mothers for the summer so we could pack and get ready to move and drive to Denver thinking when I got there and set up home I could send for him. Keith could not deal with moving away from his cousins and family. We ended up homeless in LA for nine months living in my van. I finally found another job and saved my money. Whenever I spoke to Keith about my spiritual beliefs, he at first seemed to listen. Then came a time when he thought his friends knew more and began telling me I was nuts. We were driving to a house he had to help give a bid on for a construction company he worked at. It was vacant. On the way, there he had said some hateful things about my classes and my spiritual beliefs, and I sat in silence as we drove down the road, thinking if only he could experience some of the things I have he would believe and would not think I was nuts. As soon as I thought it I felt energy pour into me and such great love it gave me hope. We pull up to the home and Keith got out to walk around it. He disappeared around the side of the house to take measurements of the pool area in the back. After a while, I got out and called his name. There was no answer. I walked around the house and then looked in the windows. There was a field next to the house but I saw nothing out there. The energy felt rather weird and I did not like being alone looking around this house since I did not work for the company so I went back to the van and sat there wondering what to do. Finally, after about two hours it was beginning to get dark, I left and went back to his mothers. I told her what had happened and I was at a loss as to what happened to Keith and was worried. She said he would call or show up thinking he was just pulling one of his stunts. I was not so sure but did not know what else to do. The next morning Keith did call. He had been in the field all night under a tree trunk scared to death. I went back to the street and picked him up. What he told me was only believed because he was picking ticks off his arms as he told me. Had he been with another girlfriend or friends he certainly would not have had ticks on his arms. He said he had walked up the hill to take a picture of the house from that angle and look at it from that vantage point. It had been later in the afternoon when it happened. He saw something shiny and white across the field and went to investigate. When he got closer, he saw strange people in capes that scared him and he hid. I asked him what do you mean strange and all he would say is with capes and hoods on. They saw him and he was so scared he hid under a big log. They found him and by then, it was dark. He said they had a light but it was not fire and he kept referring to a small one with them that really scared him. He did not like looking at him. I asked numerous times what do you mean small one? I had never seen him so scared in all our time together. He just kept saying I do not know what that thing was. I looked at him and said you mean it was an animal? ''No, that was not an animal.'' He was afraid to even think about what it looked like for fear they would find him and he could still see it's face in his mind. That is when I realized what he had seen and that the day before I had wished for him to see what I had so he would understand and not think I was crazy. He noticed my face and said, "Did you have something to do with this?" I said," I'm not sure." I told him what I had wished and he stared at me. He said a man asked him at one point if he wanted to live and at the same time, the thought of me came to his mind. He said he asked him twice and his words, "That thing, just stared at me and looked mean." He was afraid it was going to kill him. I had never seen him so scared, but then I remembered the frrst time I had seen them. The truth is the reason they asked him if he wanted to die was that he had already developed cirrhosis of the liver in the beginning stages from drinking but he would not quit. Unfortunately, he then thought I was sending them after him. Why is it people tend to think the worst about the unknown? I only wanted him to see them so he would know I was not making it up. Things deteriorated with us and finally I was wishing for a way away from him. He would not let me go, but was treating me worse and worse. Out of the blue Jonathan calls me. He and his brother were down in LA visiting his other brother and got this number from my mom. We went to meet them that evening at a restaurant and after a couple of drinks, Keith went nuts. I left with Jonathan and his brother. I was free once more only two weeks later would discover I was pregnant. I gave birth to my daughter in Hollywood and then moved back up to Seattle.

On the return trip to Seattle I drove my van and towed a trailer with all our belongings.

We stopped at Lake Shasta and rented a room in cabins for the night. It was quiet and eerie, and I knew Prometheus was around. I had been feeling bad about moving back home and after being dumped back in my body late the next morning, I woke feeling loved and went out to smell the fir trees and felt all would be right again.

At first I stayed with my parents while looking for a job. One morning before waking, I had a lucid dream about my old friend Roxi. We had separated on bad terms the last time I saw her, and I had never spoken to her again. She asked me to forgive her all the while looking over my shoulder at someone behind me. I told her I could forgive her but I would not forget it and I no longer wanted to be around her and give her the chance of doing it again. She said, "This is the last chance you will have to forgive me." When she said that I looked at her sharply and asked her what she meant. She repeated it, looking over my shoulder at someone that no matter how hard I tried to turn around I could not. She said that this would bring us back together if I did not forgive her. I told her I did forgive her but would not change my mind about giving her another chance to do it again. She nodded and said she could only stay for a few more minutes as they would not let her say more. This was her way of letting me know that an angel was behind me and she could not say more. She and I had vowed to each other that when one of us died we would come tell the other two that there was an after life. She was fulfilling her promise and we smiled at each other. Then I woke up. I got up and went upstairs to tell my parents about my strange dream when the phone rang. Dawn the other of my two friends was on the phone, and she had just had a similar dream. She had then woke and called Roxi's mother to try and hunt remembered him and so went down to the island. He was not where I had met him and so I went looking for him. A older woman told me he was ill and in a kind of tent. I went in and he was sick in his bed. I decided I would try to heal him and so wrapped my arms around him and began giving him my energy. He woke and said, "So this is how I get you in bed with me." I laughed and held him close. I felt strangely like I knew him so well when we had only spoken a few times.

All this time whenever something was not working in my life, rather than get depressed I would study Astrology to try and figure out why these things were happening. I became a good astrologer by the time I was in my thirties and did charts for friends. In my late thirties, I started a business doing charts. It was what I had always wanted to do, but could never see how I could do it and make enough money to pay the bills too. It is ever the same dilemma with everyone on this path I think, how to live a spiritual life and help others without charging so much that the only people you can help are the rich ones. On the one hand you end up charging so much that only the wealthy can afford it when you want to help the poor also, or you end up giving your services away and can not make ends meet.

Chapter Nine

During that summer, I went out one hot day and lay in the sun. As I was laying in this magical, garden I pondered my life and why I was alive now and what I was suppose to be doing and if faeries really existed. I am sure this had a lot to do with this one guy I kept seeing on the astral plane, but I did not at this time know if they were real or I was just imagining them. I was not sure if the others I had seen when I was young were faerie or not for sure, even though that is what I thought they were. But I had seen aliens, and so this made me wonder if any of the other stories were true and if I would ever get to meet them. Where the grays faeries? Pondering this, the thought came to my mind that if they did come and take me what would happen to my daughter, as she would wake and be afraid if l were not there. I would bring her with me I decided for I loved the faerie and did not feel anything sinister about them. That night when I went to change for bed, all of my bedclothes were in need of washing. All I had left was an old, tom night shirt that did not button all the way in the front and should have been tossed in the rag box. I was not going anywhere I reasoned and no one would see me. Even as I said it, I knew I was wrong and I might want to wear the other ones as they covered more. Then I thought where did these thoughts come from and felt what I call the "pause", then flat ignored it, put them on and jumped in bed. I believe I was gone before my head hit the pillow and I was suddenly waking up on a red carpet in a grand hall with my daughter next to me. I stood up and put her behind me to one side. She said, "Mommy, where are we?" I looked around and felt like I was in a lucid dream, but in a lucid dream when you look people in the eye they do not look back at you except for maybe one or two. In other words when you are dreaming those people are for the most part props that you create to learn. When they look back, they are real and usually in your dream watching you. There were about a hundred people here behind a golden cord on one side all dressed like old English or early settlement America. They were all looking at us and I looked down and realized I was half naked and became embarrassed and then angry that who ever had brought us there had not even thought to dress us. Then I heard, "You were warned." I thought how unfair that was, and then thought ok you want a good look and stood up straight, unashamed. I figured I was not ashamed of how I looked and had done nothing wrong. Then I started looking around the room to see if there was someone I recognized, I reasoned someone must have brought us there. Then I remembered that afternoon and my wish to meet the Sidhe. My smile must have stretched my whole face, I was so happy I was almost in tears. I wanted to tell them I was so happy to meet them but no one spoke, they just stared at me. There was no one in this group that looked familiar except an old gentleman in the middle of the crowd that looked remotely like Benjamin Franklin, but I had never had any thoughts of him so let that go. At the end of the hall, there was a line of people and in the middle of the people was what looked to me like Anubis. I had heard the faerie had a grand procession and dressed up so I thought for a moment that this must be a masked ball, only no one else seemed to have a costume on. I stared, and stared at him, and finally said, "Amber, what is that at the end of the hall down there?" I pointed where I meant and she looked and said, "You mean the guy with the wolf head on?" "Yes" I answered, "Only is that a mask?" I asked. "I wish I could see better, he is so far away." No sooner had I said it, than I found myself floating in front of him. Thinking to myself, "This is real, that has to be a mask, it is not a mask, come on it has to be." Thought after thought ran through my head trying to make sense of what I was looking at. I floated all around in front of him first on his left and then on his right so I could see he was not wearing a mask. It was not a mask. I looked Anubis in the eye and saw his eyes move and apologized for staring saying, "I am so sorry to stare but I never in my wildest dreams thought you were real, I mean I thought you wore a mask." Then I felt bad for saying that. I heard someone ask me, "Is he evil then?" I frowned focusing on him, and turned around and looked at the room full of beings and wondered who was talking to me. I looked back at him, and thought what a rude thing to ask me and wondered how he felt about the question being asked about him . I did not want to just trespass and read him thinking he might take it as an insult, and he was very intimidating looking from this close. I turned back to the crowd, not knowing who to address and said, " I will have to look deep into him to tell this." I was answered immediately with, "Do so then." I turned and looked him in the eye once more wondering how he felt about this. I looked deep inside, and said, "No, he is not evil, you mean because of the way he looks?" "Evil isn't because of the way you look, it is because of what you do." "Anyone can commit an evil action, that does not make them evil only the action." "Anyone can make a mistake." Then I asked whom I was talking to again. I floated back to where my daughter was and had seen someone walking around her. I calmed her down and told her that they would not hurt her as long as I was there. Then once again I asked, "Who is talking to me? Show yourself." I saw a King sitting on a throne and a Queen on his right at the other end of the great hall. For some reason the thought that I should address the King first or he might feel as if I were going to attack his Queen, it was a strange thought for me but that is what ran through my mind. I looked at him. He seemed so far away again and I wondered why I was having trouble seeing them as I had great eyesight. Again, I was floating up in front and then next to him. He stood up and turned so he was standing in front of me with his back to everyone else. I smiled, as he was so beautiful. I did not know what to say he was so beautiful. I finally said, "Well you are just,just all that." I had never used that slang term in my life and now felt stupid, but I could not think of anything to describe his beauty accurately. He did not move one muscle, just stared at me. I thought well that's ok I am staring at them. Still he did not smile. I began laughing because I was getting bombarded with energy the like of which I had never felt before, and still he did not smile, which made me laugh more. He had the best poker face I have ever seen in my life. He had long blond wavy hair to his waist and any woman alive would love to have it. His face was masculine but" without a beard effeminate somewhat. He was much taller than me had a vest that was open showing his skin. I could see the muscles in his arms and he was wearing a type of knickers that were off white. Then I heard the voice ask me if he was evil. I looked at him and all I could get out was, "You?", in the midst of my laughter. It almost seemed absurd to ask. Here was the opposite situation in a way. Anubis was ferocious looking like he could tear you in two and this King was so beautiful he was breath taking. He was intimidating with such beauty and at the same time there was an energy about him that had a sexual feeling but I believe it was Kundalini energy in me at being so close to a powerful being. What I felt was that I wanted to grab this hunk and make mad passionate love to him right then and there and I could not understand why the feelings were so strong. I was literally having a hard time controlling my own impulses he was so beautiful and was afraid I was going to embarrass myself further and grab the King. I finally just asked him, "Is it pheromones?" through all my giggles, " Is that why I am so turned on by you?" Again he ignored my question and asked me if he was evil? Then I looked down embarrassed and I said, "I do not know I would have to look you in your eyes to know." He said, "Go ahead if you dare." I had to look after he said that, but I was having the hardest time wiping the smile off my face. He was not making it any easier either as he was not even smiling in fact he was almost glaring at me as though he was trying to look as evil as he possibly could. I looked deep into his eyes, had to pull away, and looked at his chin. So much power there I felt I could just dissolve, and I heard, "But is he evil?" "No" I said. "I do not sense evil here, power yes but not evilness." Then I found myself back next to my daughter. About that time, I was exhaling and feeling like I had just been tested. I looked at the Queen and she had risen and was leaving and I thought "Doesn't she care?" She smiled as though she had a heard me, and I thought, "How could you not care?" She paused in her stride and laughed and then continued out of the room. She is very beautiful with her hair pulled up into a twist. Then my daughter was tugging on my sleeve again saying she was afraid of the big one. I said, "It's ok I see him down there, he will not get you." She is in tears and says, "No Mommy, not that one, there are two of them, the one behind us." I looked behind me and he was standing about four feet from me looking down at me. He was so tall that I had to look up to see his face. It was Set. Now Set is the only one that truly struck me as an alien. I mean his head is not any animal that we see on present day Earth. I stared again. His head looks kind of like a giraffe with square ears and red hair that color, but not quite. He seemed irritated that I was staring at him and was mouthing something at me almost like he was cursing me, and so I apologized once again. I then heard the same refrain, "Is he evil?" I looked at him and looked into his eyes. He was different. He was afraid I was going to say he was evil I think because he is different and had committed an evil act once long ago and he knew I knew this and was afraid I would say he was evil because of it. He seemed to be getting really upset and mouthing something at me, I backed up a step, and again I was asked is he evil? I said, "No, but I'm not sure why he's so upset as I've already apologized for staring." When I was finished his face changed from angry to perplexed and he pondered me. It was then that I remembered reading somewhere that redheads were related to Set and I looked at his hair. I smiled and he was reading me and seemed to relax. I looked back up at the King and he was talking to someone behind a curtain but I could never see who it was.

I could hear in my mind him talking. He said, "See, why does he send her to me when he knows I can not have her!" At the same time, I believe I felt his emotions about the situation because I almost wanted to cry. He was speaking about Jehovah I felt and I screamed, "No, he wouldn't do that, we're missing something." I felt strange energy then and decided I would wrap, only when I went to wrap I could not feel any energy. I thought that is strange and waved my hand again but it seemed as thought there was a damping field on is all I can think of. Then I was waking up sitting up in my bed, my daughter was in hers, and she was crying. I called to her and met her in the hall and she slept in my bed that night. I asked her why she was crying and she remembered the Anubis' wolf head. I told her it was ok, we were back. We went to bed and it was not until I mentioned the dream a few years later she reminded me of Set. I had forgotten him and maybe that is what he had been mouthing, a spell to make me forget. Yet, we had the same dream and woke from it at the same time. Only I do not believe it was a dream... It would be a few more years until I figured out who the King and Queen was, and that I really had been tested. Even so, I still feel quite honored that I did meet what I refer to as the Sidhe.

I was always talking to my teacher, Rama and my guide Prometheus telepathically but I did not get to see them very often physically. As you can imagine, when you first really begin using telepathy this tends to cause feelings of insecurity in you especially when you are using telepathy to talk to them. At one point, I asked Prometheus if since he had a ship could he come, pick us up, and take us for a ride. Just thinking I had the nerve to do this still makes me laugh, but I felt like I had never asked for much, so why not. Within a few days, I found myself a little more tired than usual, so I went to bed a little early. As soon as I hit the pillow I was gone. I woke in a seat on board a ship that to me seemed like a shuttle. To my right and slightly behind me was my teacher and I turned and smiled, completely excited to see him. He seemed perplexed about being there and I thought that maybe he was angry with me for asking. Suddenly I realized that if he was sitting here with me then where was Prometheus? I turned around, and looked at the back of the driver. He looked like a human from the back at first and I stared until he turned and faced me and I felt this overflowing joy. He thought, "Don't let on that you can see me or I will get into trouble." I did not answer and did not need to. In that small exchange, I was told that frequently people would see grays and not realize it because they have changed shape. I turned and looked at my teacher as if I had just spoken to another human and had not been face to face with a gray. I would not have gotten him in trouble for the world. He was my friend, guide, confidant and teacher, and had saved me numerous times I was sure.

He was doing this to give me a bit of happiness and help me realize that it really was happening and I really was talking to them telepathically. He has always been a dear heart to me. I looked out the side window in the ship and could see Highway 167 that goes through Kent. We were traveling North and parallel to it, and so low I could not understand how no one could see us. I pointed at it and said that is the way to my house. Rama asked me how that was and I said, "Well you go down there a ways and there is a clover leaf and you go around and then down further and you are there." " How?", he said. I looked out the front and could not tell how they were driving as it looked like a wormhole to me off star trek. It seemed like it was reversed like looking at a negative and it seemed like we were moving through pudding that looked like stars. I stared at it for a minute and asked, "How can you see where you are going?" Prometheus said, "Look closer" and so I did and fell into it and landed in my bed sitting up. I sat there for about thirty seconds listening and then jumped up, donned my robe, ran outside, and looked up. I could see nothing though and then heard, "Go back you can't see us, go back inside and to bed."

How do you sleep when you are so happy? He had done this for me and for no other reason than because I had asked.

I stopped eating meat at this time and decided to try to raise Kundalini again. I would still fix meat for my children, but for me I only ate vegetables and rice or potatoes. I was off work looking for a new job and meditating a lot. I did not think about it really, I just did it. The kids were in school during the day and rather than get depressed looking for a new job, I sent out resumes at the beginning of the week and then I would meditate. I received a call from a friend one day that my old teacher was in town that week for a book signing and wondered if I wanted to go see him. Of course I did, I told her and made arrangements that night for my sister to watch my daughter on Saturday. It was at the University bookstore and I arrived early so was looking around when a younger man came walking in that had the same feel as my teacher. I stood there and watched him wondering who he was. Then news reporters came in-and stood to the side. A few moments later my teacher came in and walked over to the table to get ready to sign books for people. I stood there watching him. I knew he knew I was standing there but was not looking at me, so I finally thought, "Helloooo", as loud as I could think it. He immediately looked up and scanned the crowd and stopped at my face, smiling. Rama was one of the few people I have ever been able to carry on conversations with telepathically. No matter where he was in the world, I could find him. As I gazed at him and he gazed back at me, it was as though time stopped.

He reached into his energy field after a few moments and threw a ball of energy that hit me in the third chakra and suddenly I could not wipe the smile off my face. He waved me over to him and I walked up and bought two of his books and had him sign it for me and one for my sister. We spoke briefly and I wished that we had more time together just to walk in a park by a lake and talk. That was not to be though. All of his students loved him.

People who did not know him did not understand this, but then most people do not understand what enlightenment is and when they come up against it, they are frightened. Humanity tends to think that if a person has the ability to do anything then they will, and they become afraid. It is their own lack of honor that they fear though and project onto others, or sometimes it is their inability to control people that scares them. If they can not control you then you must be out of control right? If they can do anything they want then what is going to stop them from being dishonorable? The answer, are you all listening? The answer is that they do not want to come back down in vibration. Jesus was enlightened and look what it got him from his own people. As a child I never could understand how they could kill a master, it makes no sense at all. The masters are in touch with energy and answers that could help, and has helped humanity evolve. Yet people out of control of their egos, allow this to happen over and over again. Not too smart if you see this as an evolutionary milestone for humanity, to allow it to keep happening.

While I lived there in Magnolia, I asked Prometheus about the degrees in Astrology. I had read that the original way of using them had been lost when Alexandria had burned down during a Roman war, and they only had a minimal understanding of how they were intended to be used. He showed me one way for them to be used that personalized each degree in the chart for you based on your Ascendant. I began using it with a few peoples charts and was getting good feed back on it from them. Sometimes they would ask me how I knew whatever it was I had said, and if it said that in the chart. At one point while looking at Seattle's chart, I discovered a point that when aspected I thought might set off an earthquake. Well I was wrong, but when it was aspected a certain computer company would be in the paper every time. Not having their chart I never did find out why. I began trying to write a program for the point system I was developing so I would not have to do it all by hand every time I did a chart for someone, but found that writing it in the program I had was not working the way I wanted it to. I went out and bought a book on the computer language Plus, but could never get interested enough in it or find the time to work on it uninterrupted.

I wondered what Rama felt like physically and mentally if he was hyped constantly from so much energy pouring into him. He had been enlightened for so long in body that I wondered how he did it and what he felt like. My two experiences with Kundalini rising had been very short lived and I could not imagine how he could continue it in this world. One day the energy in me rose to my heart chakra and stopped there. I felt like from my heart chakra down was wide open. This lasted for a week or so and I felt nauseous off and on like when you are extremely horny and no one around to placate it. Yes boys, women do feel that way too. I tried eating Tumms but it did not help. It felt like there was a constant stream of energy coming into my second and third chakra. It did not feel negative other than it was making me extremely horny. The only time I felt at ease was when I meditated, and. then I could just drop into position and soar. One day I was watching TV with my kids and stretched back trying to alleviate the feeling in my stomach like you would a sore muscle. Quite suddenly I felt like someone dove into me and the energy charged up into my mind and my crown was wide open. Immediately I sat up again and then the smile came.. .l felt him in me and I turned and looked at my son and heard in my mind and with my own ears my voice saying my son's name and knew it was not me that had said it. Sherman smiled and looked at me wondering why I was chuckling, for a moment I felt like I was in the background watching. Sherman had met him when he was four.

I realized that they would think I had lost my mind and said "nothing, never mind", and got up and walked into the bathroom. I had asked what he felt like and was being shown. Everything I looked at took on this surreal light that made it look even more alive and there was white noise or rather I was experiencing everything making noise louder than normal. My senses were all heightened. It was as though I was one with everything. I got up and walked in my bedroom and lay down on my bed to try and pull myself together and get used to it a little before I tried to interact with anyone else. I could feel this other consciousness in me. It was not scary, and by that I mean I did not feel out of control or that I was being possessed. He just waited for me to get it together, and I tried because I thought it was a great opportunity. I laid there on my bed and tried to get the energy to tone down a bit so I could feel more at ease, it did not work. Then I tried just letting it flow and going with it. What a rush. I could only deal with it for what seemed like ten minutes; the rushing of thoughts and the answers coming at me so fast made me laugh. Just knowing things I would have no way of knowing, and the worst thing was I could not wipe the smile off my face. Every time a thought's answer came to me, at the same time I could imagine the expressions of people wondering how "I" knew it and it struck me as hilarious. I was so far out there and I was afraid that there would be no one around to help me do for myself, somehow I could not see driving like this. Your focus is so broad, in that you are seeing so much at once that it seemed difficult to focus on details, although many do. It could be that this was just my fears(ego) bubbling up to the surface, but it would definitely be a whole new learning curve. I could not afford a servant or butler like he had. I was the only one to take care of my kids. I felt responsible for them and would not ask for others to raise them from my family because they had chosen me for a parent, not my family. Again my own ego was trying to bring me down fearing for it's very life. I reached for a cigarette to pull myself together, and he said, "If you smoke with me in here, I will have to leave." I could not deal with it longer though with my kids there and said, "I can not do this any longer," and immediately he was gone. Then my phone rang and a man's voice on the other end said, "Arna, Aima, Marah", and I asked who it was and he hung up. I have no idea who it was, but he had an accent. Who ever it was knew exactly what had just transpired with me.

I tried to quit smoking after that. After three days of not having a cigarette, I began hearing his voice telepathically again. He would answer my thoughts. I knew it was not me, but it was very unnerving and I finally decided I would walk down to the comer store and buy some cigarettes. I walked out the door feeling like I was being watched and chided myself for it. I get to the comer and there are the strangest two people I have ever seen in the small conservative community I lived in. Not only did they look strangely dressed, but almost feral like street kids from the East Coast and they certainly did not belong there. I went in the store, bought the cigarettes and walked out. They were still at the comer and I felt like I did not even want to walk by them. The vibrations coming from them were alien feeling and I was not sure what they might do. So I took a short cut across some grass to avoid them. I walked up the block and a limozine pulled out of a space on a side street where he had been parallel parked and pulled up beside me. I stopped waiting for the windows to come down. It sat there for the longest time and I could not see who was in it but I could feel them and the high energy. I looked at the driver whom I could see and smiled and asked him if I could help him with something. He looked in his rear view mirror, smiled but said, "No, not this time", then drove off. That really irritated me because I was pretty sure it was my teacher in the back seat and I could not figure out why he would go to so much trouble to come see me and not even speak to me. I walked back to my home and as I walked into the dining room I hear in my mind, "you have gained weight." Then I knew it was him. It was the same thing I had thought when I frrst met him after having only seen his picture on his first book. It had become a joke almost between us. This time I was irritated though because I had gained weight from trying to quit smoking. It was my dearest wish to just walk with him in a park by some water and talk, yet I was never to get that wish, at least not on this plane. It was as though he was forcing me to accept learning from him telepathically in this way so I could progress further and faster. Trust myself and my intuition. He was trying to help me remember who and what I am.

I had another dream after this where I became lucid in a room with nothing but a table in it. There was a door on the far wall from me and to my left what looked like a card table. On top of it were what looked to me like short swords, wands, and various other magical items. As I was looking them over the door suddenly burst open and in walked my teacher, Rama and four other students. The students walked up in front of me facing me and Rama stood on my right. A young woman in front of me glanced at him and I heard him tell her to hand me the sword she was holding telepathically. She then handed me the long sword point first. I could hear Rama's intake of breath next to me as he read my thoughts as I snatched it out of her hands so fast and whipped it around and over my arm hilt first and handed it back to her saying, "This is how you hand someone a sword, otherwise they might think you are threatening them." She looked at him, wondering if she should take the sword back, and I too turned and looked at him for another reason. I had heard his thought with the intake of breath, he was afraid I was going to take it as a threat and attack her, and I was surprised that he thought I would do this to a young novice. I woke up after this and pondered it for a while. I could not understand why Rama could not "read" me well enough to know I would not

do that. I feel it is my soul and it's instinctive quality that

moves so fast that they can not read it, still it amazes me

that he could not. It was so obvious to me that he was not

sure, and I was left to ponder how this could be.

Chapter Ten

Rama had made a point of saying sometimes as students on the path we would get tired of dealing with the hubris of work or relationships and become a hermit for a while and then after a break would be back into life again. Such was happening to me, but not because I wanted to get back into mainstream living again, but because I had to be responsible and make a living and support my children. If it had been my choice I would have done charts for people, or done some form of art work. I did not understand then how to make these positions work in a material way.

I went to back to work doing payroll. I had tried starting a business doing Astrology charts and still had it going, but could not make enough money at it to pay the rent. I could have if I wanted to do a less than an ideal job to me, and only give them some information. Or I could just print out a computer generated interpretation for them. The computer printouts had actually taken on much better quality at this time, but I wanted to put my all into the charts I did. Give them the benefit of my knowledge and study and let them know what I saw by way of what their soul had come into this life for and a computer print out could not do that. I did do this for many friends, but it took me about a week to really dive into their charts, find the key I was looking for and have their chart open up for me. In this way I could tie much of their life together and actually help them answer the "why am I here" question we have all had at one time or another. Those I did do charts for usually came back to me and let me know how accurately I had seen some things in their life. I told them to hold onto it and the next time they were feeling down pull it out and see if it helped them understand what was going on. Some did this and came back to me six months to a year later and wanted transits done or to know more. For me it was just plain fascinating how it all pulled together and they had planned out their lives to help them evolve. Still even with my new position and doing charts I was still not making enough to take care of bills and so had to move my home. While I was looking for places I realized that nothing in Seattle would be low enough rent wise to allow me to get caught up, so I would have to move out of the city. I ended up in the area that I had seen on the ship that evening with Prometheus and my teacher. It was a long drive to work and back each night and being in an apartment with people partying all night below me was just not good when you have to get up early for work. It was no fun. The only nice thing was I had a deck that looked out onto a wooded area. I put most of my plants on the back deck that faced south as it was the only place in my apartment that could be open to the sun. Leaving the curtains open made the whole place hot. While here I worked on my astrology and meditated. I also had a daughter who was in 4th grade and needed to keep an eye on her. Where this book is not about my everyday, what I would call normal life, I thought I should mention I really did have one. It was just more magical than most peoples, or maybe I was just more aware of the magic in my life. For instance driving in from Kent to Seattle everyday I seemed always to be in traffic. Often I would tune into my teacher where ever he was in the world and talk telepathically. This was not unusual for me at all and by this time in my life I actually looked forward to it. He was one of the few people I have ever been able to carry on a conversation with telepathically to so it made me feel connected in a special way and not alone. One day as I sat in what I refer to as the fast lane, (anyone from California will understand this but for those who are not, it is the left hand lane not counting any HOV lane), in traffic at a crawl, I felt his mind. I say felt, because everyone has a different feel to them and just as if someone touched you physically, even if you had your eyes closed, if you were close to them you would know who it was. So the feel of him was so strong I chuckled and looked in my rear view mirror and sure enough there was the limo coming up in the HOV lane. I thought, "Well that is nice, here I am stuck in this traffic and he gets to cruise through, that is not fair." About that time a strange thing happened. I saw a police officer about two cars back from me and thought how funny it would be if the officer pulled them over. The police car flew out into the HOV lane behind them with his siren on and I really do not know how the limo driver missed him, but the officer must have realized what he had done, as then the limo jumped over where the officer had been and around him going from the HOV to the fast lane and back again to the HOV lane. I realize that my thoughts are seeming to somehow affect what is happening and I have my hand over my mouth and am laughing as the limo passes me slowly, very slowly. I could feel his eyes on me. It was not funny in the least but I could not stop laughing at the thought that I had just caused that. He drove off ahead and traffic finally picked up so we began to move. At the time I worked close to the Seattle Center and so got off at Mercer and drove over by Westlake. There pulled off the road is the limo, seemingly waiting for me. I pulled off and sat there for a moment thinking whether I should approach it or not. Finally I decided against it as I was already late to work and drove off. Later as I went out front door of the building I worked in, to take a break, who but the same limo pulls up to a light and even though it changed to green it still sat there. At times like this I always wondered what if it is not him and I go open the door to this limo and it not be him, and the people freak. So I refrained, but I have regretted doing so. Once I had a boyfriend with a brown Porche Carerra. It was the only brown one I had ever seen. One evening I was on my way over to his place on top of Mount Tamalpais and this brown Porche flies by me. I am driving an old Ford Falcon. Thinking it is my boyfriend I try to keep up. For a couple of miles I am right on this guy. Finally we come to a stop sign and the guy turns around and looks at me so I can see him. It was not my friend. I yelled sorry at him and left embarrassed beyond belief but laughing at the whole incident. I could not help but imagine what that poor guy thought about a seemingly wacko woman driving behind him trying to catch him in an old Ford Falcon.... Ha Ha Needless to say I was not going to do it again even if the limo sat there till another car came up behind it and it had to move.

Which it did. This was just one incidence, but there were many during this time. Always I could feel the occupant, always I would tum in the direction of the feeling and there it would be. As I write this I can only hope that those who have similar experiences release your inhibitions and go for it. So many of societies ways inhibit natural evolution of abilities. Listen to you intuition, so what if your ego gets a little embarrassed some times. The other side of the coin is you will experience magic at it's best, and there is nothing better. I went and saw Rama one night while I was meditating and remote viewing and found him in bed curled up asleep. It takes a while when you first begin remote viewing to trust that what you are seeing is not your imagination. He was on the east coast and I was on the west coast so for him it was the middle of the night. I could see him so clearly and he looked so sweet like a little boy all curled up sleeping and I did not want to wake him. I kept getting this urge to go over and give him a kiss on the cheek before I left, and it was simply unbearable, and the thought kept running through my mind like I would not get another chance like this, and so I bent down to kiss his cheek. He turned over and kissed me back and so surprised me I jerked myself out of meditation. He had been awake the whole time. This opened a whole different world to me. Not only did it exercise my focus, which it takes a lot of to accomplish, but I was having loads of fun. All work should be so fun. There will always be those great loves in your life that you can think about and they call, or in thinking about them you almost feel like you can hear them answering you. They are, or a part of them is. A part of them is answering you and that is why they sometimes call. That is the magic between you. Your minds(spirits) are connected in a way others are not and their spirit is answering you. You are on the same wave length. I used to experience this with another friend of mine and it got to the point that he would call me and laughingly say, "quit thinking of me." For the most part, in many cases it is the spirit of the person in question that you are conversing with and their consciousness knows nothing of it. I say this because in most instances the conscious personality of the person will not be aware of what is happening. They may not be aware of what you discuss with them on the astral but they may vaguely have a funny feeling about you. I do feel it is a necessary item for humanity to learn about as we are moving towards the changing of the ages and the lifting of veils to be aware of so they do not experience it inadvertently and not understand what is happening. Very important. As the veils begin to thin, I for one feel it is extremely important for people to learn meditation, or Tarot, or some form of getting in touch with your own inner self. In doing so you open yourself to understanding of different dimensions, opening your chakras and with them your intuition.

It was while I lived in Kent that I learned about Kabala. While taking actual classes from him years earlier I had asked him what I was and who I was that I was able to do some of the things I've done. He told me then to read up on Kabala and look into what my name meant, that he could not remember what my name meant exactly but thought there were a few goddesses with· that name, so one of them could have something to do with me. So I bought my first book on the subject and it made perfect sense to me. What I saw though was a system left by beings from other worlds that humanity saw as angels and gods to help humanity one day get back in touch with them. Since I could already go into deep meditation and remote view I found this easy. I was soon walking the tree nightly just to talk to the beings up there. It was here that I discovered what my name meant. Janet or in this language it would be Jahnets meaning Jehovah's flower.

When Rama had asked me years earlier he had made me repeat my name over and over because I did not always say it the same. The majority of the time I said, Ja-nut which would mean Jehovah's sky goddess, but other times I said Ja-nit, and Nit was another Egyptian goddess. So I settled on Jahnets because it is closer to what I grew up with in meaning. I always thought it meant Gods grace, so Gods flower is close. There is also Ja-netz which would be Jehovah's hawk, this also fits as my physical vision most of my life was 20-30 which means I can see farther off like a hawk has far vision. In Astrology, I have Mercury(detail view), Jupiter(Broad view), and Uranus (universal view) conjunct in Cancer(soul, intuition), which gives my intuition those characteristics. My sun and moon are both at 11 degrees and my Ascendant is at 7, so my numbers really are 7/11. I am bringing this up here because all my life I have been trying to find out what my soul came here for, what was my intention in this incarnation and why some of these things happen to me. I always figured that if I knew what I was suppose to be doing, I would just do it and life would be so much simpler. So when I began walking the tree as it is called, I met up with beings whom I believe humanity thought were the gods of ancient times.

The being at the position of Chokmah, I assumed was representative of Jehovah. I was wrong, but for now this is what I thought at the time. So I would go up and ask him, why me? He did not physically talk for the most part, but was telepathic, and would answer me. I would receive pictures along with telepathy that answered my questions. One day I was very frustrated with answers or lack of answers because sometimes the answers would come slowly, and I went up and asked again, why me? What is it about me that makes me so different that all this is happening to me? He was not answering again and I got very upset. I ended up yelling at him, in his face and demanding an answer. I was determined to get an answer or die trying. He stepped over to me very swiftly, with a Mona Lisa smile on his face and got really close so I could see his face very clearly and said, "I just learned something." Completely took the wind out of my sails.

That had stunned me so that I came out of meditation and sat there just thinking, with my mouth hanging open. There was no way that was just in my mind. So they learn from what we do down here as well as us learning from them. They were real... They taught and were being taught. This is when I found out that to be a teacher you also have to be a student. It has to do with polarity and balance, a student is the opposite of a teacher and you can not be one without the other. At this point I had questioned whether they were real or just part of our imagination, or as many others probably think part of our higher selves. I think this is a very healthy thing to do with anything occult. Up until this point I thought they were part of my inner self. But he had just interacted with me and there would be no going back to any thoughts that this could be my imagination. Your imagination does not interact with you on this level like another being, and no I am not split personality. In fact I am not at all sure I even believe you can be.

Many things happened during this time span to me. As I was driving to work one day rather upset that I had to deal with normal life at all, a golden hawk flew down right in front of my window on the freeway. I took my foot off the peddle in fear he would splatter on my windshield and he turned and looked me in the eye at that split second. It was so beautiful that it changed my whole demeanor for the day. I could not help but smile all day. I felt honored by this bird. I would meet up with him years later at my home again. Another interesting thing that happened to me during this period happened when I was on my way home from work. As far as abilities I had not done anything unusual for many years and I mentioned this to Chokmah while pondering all this information he was giving me. There is a stretch of freeway called 405 that travels overhead and across the valley as though it is a bridge. I was on this one evening driving home after work and the sun had not set yet. Another woman was two lanes over from me on my left and slightly ahead of me. Suddenly from out of nowhere a dog climbs the guardrail onto the freeway. I was stunned that the dog could even get up there. It took off across the freeway almost directly in front of the other woman and both her and I hit our brakes, and I screamed "No" as I did not want to see this poor dog squished at 60 mph. I also did not want him to get drug under her car and so "saw" him rising up. I saw the dog rise and kept pulling my head back almost as if to help it rise so that when the car hit him, he only bounced very slightly and rolled as she had slowed down some. We had both stopped our cars at this point and the traffic behind us I guess witnessing this had also stopped. I thought "here". The dog then ran straight across three lanes, over to my car like it knew me. I looked down at it opened my door and said, "Get in the back and sit down." It did just what I said and I closed the door and both the woman in the other car and I took off as though nothing had just happened. The other woman mouthed Thank You to me and I nodded and smiled at her as she headed towards Bellevue and I took the freeway to Kent. Once home I found a veterinary and asked if they would just check him to make sure he did not have internal bleeding and none would without me paying them. At this time in my life I had no money to pay them as they all wanted outrageous amounts. I finally ended up taking him to the pound as I lived in an apartment and could not have a dog.

It was a white and red haired Springer spaniel. When I got
to the pound the attendant said he had been chasing this
same dog earlier and he had gotten away from him. He had
owners, but the dog kept escaping the yard. He checked
him over and said he seemed to be doing fine and did not
think he had internal bleeding. It was one of the hardest
things I have ever done to turn him over to the pound after
just saving his life, and I cried all night.

Prometheus had gone back to his planet while I lived in
the apartment and I had Jehovah or who I thought was him,
and my teacher to keep me company. I purchased a book
on Lilith to learn more about her for Astrology but did not
count on what would happen. For the first time in my life I
felt Jehovah had done something wrong to Lilith and I was
tom. I felt like my faith was being shredded and could not
understand why he had done what he did. I went to him
and told him that it was imperative that I understand this.
How could he be her consort and still allow Adam to treat
her not as an equal and to be beneath him?

1bis was to be the first time I was shown the answer
in such a way that I felt the answer. It took a few weeks

to get my answer and during that time our relations became strained. I felt it was because I had questioned him and he thought my faith had wavered. It really had not though because in my heart I knew he had to have a good explanation and so waited for it, reminding him of my question every so often. He finally said, "I do not want to hurt you."

Puzzled, my imagination took over and all sorts of possible answers began running through my mind. The most plausible was that he was jealous somehow but that did not set well with me either. For he had used her to get Adam going while Adam had not known which end was up. He had used her because she turned him on and so should be able to handle Adam. After all Adam was him once removed. So jealousy did not fit. After a day of every possible reason I could think of, I finally went up and confronted him once more. He finally asked me who Shekhina was, and I said, ''the Earth Goddess.'' He nodded and asked me where she was in relation to Adam. Suddenly pictures and answers began pouring into my mind. He stands on her, she is earth, so she is technically beneath

him, she will never be equal to him because she is "more"
than him. Is not the Earth more than human? How can the
Goddess be equal to man? She supports man, without her
he would fall. Once more I had been shown that they look
at things in an entirely different manner than humans.
Lilith being down on Earth with Adam was confused and
looking at it in a manner akin to how a human looked at
things. But she was not human and he could not make her
equal with them without hurting her. Humans are props,
bodies. The spirits and souls incarnate into bodies to work
out issues with each other. It is quicker on the material
plane to learn and work them out for a being who is pure
intellect and a being who is pure instinct and emotion.
Just like I will ask a question and it takes weeks to get an
answer from them, sometimes years, they are not ignoring
us like Lilith and all the other female souls thought. It
takes time to manifest the perfect answer here, but when
it does it is instantaneous in your mind like someone
flipped a switch and you understand. When the Shekhina
is in exile, this means she is incarnated in body and has
not remembered her true nature yet. While she is waking

up so to speak, her astral body is his consort. Her astral body came to Adam to help him and Adam could not help himself, beholding a goddess. Frequently spirits would fall so far in consciousness down to the Earth that they took on the shapes of their linage, that is where the birds feet, wings, bulls horns, lions claws, horses hoofs and some even half and half came from. They are our lineage too, because we are spirit and soul both. The spirit is shape shifter and can be anything or appear as anything it wants to be. Kind of gives you a whole other view of not eating meat and why Jehovah/Al/El thought all should be destroyed due to cannibalism.

Then one day I asked Rama about Jehovah. He asked me to describe him and I did. He just stood there pondering what I had just said, and I asked him if he wanted to go up and see him. So we did go to the place I went to talk to him. Rama bowed to the ground and stayed there, and I thought, "Am I being disrespectful not bowing", to myself but when I went to bow and follow suit Jehovah stopped me and said you do not have to do that. It is his way to show me respect, but I know you respect me already. That was strange. To have my teacher whom I respected bowing and yet I did not have to. I was not sure what to make out of it, and again I wondered if I was being egotistical. Just one more puzzling think that would take years to understand. It was one more way for him to tell me what I was and answer my question only I could not accept it without feeling egotistical.

This was taking place in the first part of 1998. A few days before Easter, Rama came and spoke to me one night. We talked all night. It was great. I felt like I was glowing when I went to Easter dinner with my relatives and they even commented on it asking me if l had a new boyfriend. That night when I got home I went to see him in meditation, only Jehovah was there too. He said he was going to have to take Rama and he did not want me upset by it so he wanted me to know first hand. I asked why and he said that Rama could not go back to what he was before, he had to go on because it was too painful. I then went to talk to Rama. He asked me to let him go, that he was in pain and he had to leave. It was so hard to do and I cried knowing there would be no one on this plane that truly understood me, but I somehow found the strength and watched his eyes close. He looked whiter than his usual self and seemed to be wearing white robes. Then when I left him and went down to my normal place on the astral I saw Jehovah above me, reach out and take him with what looked like a bolt of white energy that was curved like a rainbow only without the colors. When I woke the next day, I thought it must be in my imagination. It is very difficult seeing this in your mind and not thinking in our society that this was just my imagination and then wondering why on earth I would think such a thing about someone I loved so much. I just could not accept what I saw happening as actual reality. I did not want to accept it. When I went to see him, he seemed far away. Like an old time long distance phone call is the best way I can describe it. I asked him where he was and he was evasive about it. The next day we went on talking as normal only he seemed really concerned about something, but he was not saying what. Finally I received a phone call two weeks after Easter that he had passed from physical existence on Easter. I said that can not be I have been talking to him every day. They said others of his students had been doing the same. We all

knew that we are not our bodies, but we had experienced it

in a way not many do. We experienced it like the disciples

experienced it with Jesus. He had come back this lifetime

to teach women and try and change what had happened to

what he had taught the first time. He was not gone at all.

His spirit was still with all of us because he had become

enlightened while on earth so he was just free of the body.

Still I was really upset for months. My heart was broken.

I literally felt it leak when I found out. I could not leave

though because I had a child that was still to young to take

care of herself. My grief was so strong that it took me a long

time to get over his being gone. I am sure it is the same

for the rest of his students too. It is hard to be so close to

a master and have him leave, even though I knew he was

not gone. Physically he was, his body was gone, but his

spirit was still here with me talking to me and I am sure his

other students too. Helping us all through this grief so we

could help others in the future. Then I was let go at work.

It was crummy the way it was done, but it gave me time

to grieve and get myself together about it. So everything

does happen for a reason. I also found out that there was a girl there who had gone into a coma when he died. I went into meditation and went and saw her while she was in the coma. I did not know her, or even what she looked like, but I did not want Rama to have more Karma because of her. I told her that if she truly loved him as much as she said she would live out her life. Life is not meant to be thrown away. It is a gift. Rama was enlightened and so simply walked out of his body and let it go. She was not enlightened yet and it would not be the same. I tried and that is all I could do. Two days later I received a call that she had come out of the coma the day before. Who knows, but when it keeps happening to you all your life then you can decide. I do not believe in coincidence anymore. Then I got sick with strep throat and had no insurance or money to go to the doctor. I was very sick and laying on my living room couch one night because I was so hot I could not sleep. I finally passed out from exhaustion only waking to see him standing at the end of the couch. He reached down and grabbed me right at the throat area as if grabbing my shirt collar and literally pulled me up off the couch and said, "what are you doing?" Then he threw me back down on the couch, with me grumbling that I had finally gotten to sleep and why was he waking me. The next morning I felt much better but went to the doctors anyway. Then one day he told me he had to leave for a while and be alone to go over his life. He told me Jehovah would be there for me if l needed anyone, and he was there for me, and we talked like Rama and I had talked for hours at night. Then I said I had to stop and think about all this in my life. He told me he would be there for me when and if l needed him. That was good.

Chapter Eleven

I began looking for a new job and working on my astrology. My daughter found someone to take her bird that was in heat and driving us nuts with it's constant whistling. Across the hall from them was a guy I met with more birds and we after a time ended up getting together. I felt it was what I needed at the time to focus more on physical reality and forget about my grief. I found another job and about a year and a halflater we began looking for a place together. I got upset one day because I had found a place I wanted and called on it and was told they were selling it to a developer to tear down. It was a great old home with a wrap around porch. It had character which many of the new places did not. I was so upset about this my boyfriend grabbed the paper and found another place close by that we could go look at. It was very expensive but when we called the man said we could come over to look. It was May 5th of 2000 at 5:55 pm. It was beautiful. Exactly what I had always wanted and I felt from the time I walked on the property that I had been given this place. This was magic. Even the owner that sold it felt the same way. I was an astrologer and so was he. I loved the trees and the garden and was obviously in heaven walking around it. I had excellent credit so it was no problem for me to get the loan. It was the garden I had always wanted. Some years later I would discover it was a copy of the place I go to on the astral plane only from the back looking forward, which is interesting in itself as it is like a half plane away. The only thing that is missing is one tree and strangely enough, it is a tree I have been trying to grow since I have been here only to have the squirrels dig up and eat the acorns, an oak. I almost bought an oak at a nursery that was going out of business up the street only I was not sure which kind of oak I wanted. It was not until I was reading a book on manifestation that I walked out back and when I turned around to come in, realized I had created this place years before and had been changing it around to suit me all this time. My home is proof we create our world with our thoughts. This can be taught to people and I believe our world would be a much happier place. People would not blame everyone else for their life being what it is as they could see how they are doing it. Oh and I am the Oak.

People were talking more and more about earthquakes in 200I, so I asked Prometheus if there was any way that my kids could be here if a big earthquake hit so I wouldn't have to worry about them. He nodded and that was the last I thought of it. Then one day my daughter got sick with what I thought was strep throat. I stayed home and made an appointment to take her in to the doctors office on her birthday. As we were getting ready a strong earthquake rolled right down our street. I was amazed we were home together like I had asked. Rama had told me that the Northwest was my place and not to be afraid because he would be with me, and he has been. Only I did not realize it was him for a few more years.

Once again I was in a relationship that began with seeming acceptance of what I could do and what I saw only to have it end up with them expecting me to just forget about everything I had learned and live life their way. As if l could just ignore what I had learned so they could be lazy and not even strive to evolve. Most people just want to get by. They do not want to make any effort to raise their consciousness or become enlightened, because it is hard work. They do not care what kind of Karma they incur or what their partner incurs because of their actions, and they do incur due to their partners actions. Remember this when you take a partner, that your Karma and theirs are taken on by each other.

It is this laziness that I feel has ruined many of my relationships, because once you know what the oneness feels like, you can never give up striving for it. It would be like having sex once and then being told to forever forget about it for the rest of your life because your mate does not believe in sex. Not for me... I would say something about what I was experiencing, and he did not want to talk about it out of fear and would change the subject. Most people get really weirded-out when I talk about occult or philosophy and expect me not to talk to them about it. That is like me not allowing them to talk about what ever is most important to them whether it be their job, hobby, or other interest. We ended up breaking up.

It was about four months later that I sat down on my couch and just cried. I felt like there was not anyone for me and no one would ever understand me and I just did not belong in this world. My teacher had left this plane and I felt alone as he was the only one I could carry on an actual conversation with telepathically. When I tried to use my talents I was branded weird by people who were afraid of their shadows. I just could not understand why I had these abilities if I could not use them, and no one listened so that I could teach them, what is the point? I knew that beings watched me and so I cried and cried until someone finally answered me. I was suddenly not on my couch or rather I was but what was in front of me was another room. A man who looked Egyptian was walking around the room and asked me, "What do you want?" I was so surprised I just stared at him wondering who he was. The idea of God popped into my mind and I asked him if he was Jehovah? He said he had been known by that "title" at one time. Now I am sure my mouth was on the floor because my brain was having a hard time comprehending how this guy who is dressed and looks like a Pharaoh could be Jehovah, and if he was, then who was the one I had met before. He turned around and walked over to pick something up off a table and I thought I need to remember as many details about this vision as possible. So I looked at his clothes and his legs and skin color, about that time I realized how good looking he was and he was mid stride walking over to the table and stopped hearing my thought and looked over his shoulder in a perfect come hither look. Then I was embarrassed and literally felt myself blush.

His hair was black and it was curly like the sculptures of the original gods in Sumer or the Hittites. It was rolled only there were no rollers and I found myself wondering how he was able to get his hair to do that. Silly thought but we think silly things at times. It was down to his hips in the back and the top half was pulled back into a pony tail and then it curled. When I began looking at him trying to remember as many details as possible he read my mind and began posing for me. As I thought of his eye color, he came up really close, eye to eye, so I could see his eyes. His eyes were changing right in front of my eyes as though they could be any color he wanted and then settled on a rusty colored brown and I was surprised at that. When I saw them changing, I thought that he was just giving me what I thought the color should be, only I would have never thought rusty brown. Then he asked me what I wanted again, face to face with his face no more than an inch away from mine. I felt like I loved my teacher and missed him, I could not understand how I was so attracted to this guy while I was so upset about my teacher and was getting very confused. I was afraid to tell him the truth because I knew somehow it would upset him, but I knew also I could not lie to him even to save his feelings. I finally said, "I want him." He looked at me for a second and then looked inwards realizing who I was referring to and disappeared and I was back on my couch. Well he had stopped my crying I thought... I never did find out who he was other than he looked like the spirit of Pharaoh Tutakamen. He did stop me from crying though, and gave me something new to ponder. It would be much later that I would figure out he was, Thoth.

Prometheus had only left a couple of times to go home and always when I was with another teacher, so I always had someone around. He had a ship and I could always see him sitting at controls and looking down at me as if through a screen. When he came into his room and sat down at the controls I would see him, feel him and acknowledge his presence. One day two males showed up there. I wondered who they were but ignored them and went to look for Prometheus. Not finding him immediately, I finally went into meditation and found him. There seemed to be activity going on around him in his ship and he seemed upset. I picked up that they had somehow found his ship and boarded it. I walked over to one of the men who looked in charge there and told him if they hurt him they would have me to deal with. He seemed confused that I would stick up for him. I reiterated that he was my friend and if he got hurt at all I would be extremely upset and he would not like it. He said he understood. Then I walked back over to Prometheus and told him that I thought he would be ok and for him to let me know if there was a problem. I knew he was in trouble and told him I would stand up for him no matter what, that he was my friend. He said, "Remember you said that when you understand more of what is going on." All of this was telepathic. I could feel that he did not think I would understand when the time came and it upset me because I loved him like family. He had always been there for me no matter what I wanted to talk about and for him to feel I would desert him hurt. I left then as I had to get ready for work, but I was upset now and wondering all day who they were. I could see them going through his ship as they walked past his console trying to figure out his controls and such. As Prometheus had taught me all my life, when I did not understand something I would go to astrology first to see if l could figure out what was going on, so when I came home from work I did this. This time as I sat there trying to figure out who these people were exactly and two of them came and sat down in Prometheus's craft at his console. One was really big and handsome and looked like the being I had known as Chokmah a few years earlier, but had darker hair that was long. He reminded me of the Annunaki the way his hair was styled and I kept an eye on them while I was studying. They kept talking about the console, and the other one a blonde guy with shoulder length hair, and in a uniform of some kind, asked the other one if he thought Prometheus talked to me through it. I found myself listening to them so much I could not concentrate on the math calculations I was doing as they were distracting me. I had never spoken to any one else this way and I was beginning to think I was going nuts, and all day had been ignoring them. When he asked that, I finally answered them saying, "Yes!" They looked at each other and at me in the console and the big guy said, "Did she just answer us?" I said, "Yes I did now if you do not mind I'm trying to get some work done here so if you could go somewhere else to talk, I'd appreciate it." That apparently was more than they expected and they jumped up and ran off the screen or out of my field of view. This was the first time that I realized for sure, that I must have had something in me to be able to see Prometheus all this time. I had always thought he was just appearing in my mind and had taken it for granted. It had never occurred to me that I was seeing him through a device because I also remote viewed so seeing him at a console really was not unusual. I sat there pondering that for a while before I went back to my transit work but I was not sure what I was looking for and the big guy had come back and was just sitting there watching me. He seemed fascinated and it was obvious that he wanted to talk but did not want to disturb me. I finally said, "Hello" to him. He asked me if I could understand him and I said yes. He seemed surprised by this and I said surely other humans can understand you! All he would say was, "Not like this." I assumed he was talking about the console. I asked him if Prometheus was ok, and he said he was being held on his ship. He asked me why I cared about him and I told him I had been talking to him a long time and he had taught me a lot. He was my teacher and I loved him like family. I finally gave up on my Astrology and dropped into meditation, left my body and went up there. It surprised him when I appeared behind him and he asked me what else I could do. I was not sure I should be giving away so much so I just said, "I can do a lot of things." I asked him if he was Annunaki and he said he was but he would not tell me his name. I found I enjoyed talking to him. He had a gentle way about him but looked somewhat like a wrestler only bigger and when his men were around I could tell they had a great deal of respect for him. We became friends somewhat and when I would ask him questions he had the most interesting way of answering me. Sometimes it would be a few days before I would get an answer so that I did not think I was going to get one. Then something would happen in my life and I would be thinking about what the person's trip was and he would pop into my minds eye and say something like, "Does that answer your question?" The first time he did it, I was astounded. He had let me feel the why of how something happened. He was very quiet but I could read how he was feeling and he was really interested in this. It seemed to bother him that I could read him so well sometimes, and he finally turned on me one day and asked me how I knew something he said was not accurate. I told him that I could feel he did not feel that way really. He said, "You are empathic," with a grin this seemed to explain something about me to him. I really enjoyed talking to him because I was learning about them on a one on one basis. It was through him that I learned that their names changed depending on what they had achieved or how they had evolved. So the same name they had whey they were young would not be the same thing when they were older and also titles were involved so their life was very hierarchal.

He told me I could call him Chokmah which is a title finally, but it was like pulling teeth to get that much out of him. He looked like the one I had met when I walked the tree years earlier only his hair was darker. I would go up and talk to him when I came home from work and meditated. I did this so much that it became easy to just kind of pause or shift my awareness to where he was and see both him, and what was going on in my dimension too. That was difficult at fust but became easier the more I did it. It was difficult only dealing with the normal people around me as they seemed to think I was day dreaming or not paying attention to them. One day I asked him about eating because someone on a list on the internet had mentioned something about food and the being they were talking to being vegetarian. I realized I had never seen him eat, so when I went to see him I asked.

I was trying to understand if they were just in another dimension or were spiritual, or is this all in my mind. The next day when I went up he had a table laid out with food for me to see and was sitting there eating when I came up. Then he asked me if I wanted some. I could not help but think about the stories of the faerie lands and if you eat there you could get stuck. Since I was not sure whether these were the Sidhe or not, I was not sure if l should eat. I asked him if it would hurt me or cause me to get stuck there and he laughed and said no. Then I said I was a vegetarian and did not eat meat and asked if it had meat in it and he told me no. So I ate it. It was the texture of lychee fruit and tasted like it too. He told me not to eat too much of it though because I was not used to it. A few days later I bought fresh lychee fruit at a store and planted the seeds and they sprouted. I had three lychee trees growing but it is too cold up here in the Northwest and I put them outside when the weather became warm and then we had a cold front and they died.

The next time I went up there, many others were there with him eating. He had me sit down by him on cushions and there was a long table there in a sunken area in the great hall in front of his throne. One of his men tossed him something I thought was food and I saw this out of my peripheral vision and reached up and snatched it out of the air and ate it. They both looked at me and I laughed and said, "You did not think I was that quick did you?" The look on their faces seemed to say mistake and I asked, "What, I can not have any of that?" He only said you should not have eaten that because you are not used to it and it may keep you awake for a long time. Sure enough, I tossed and turned all night unable to sleep like I had drank 20 cups of coffee. Finally I went up and saw him and he kept me company in his round bed all night. Every once in a while an experience like this one would happen where I would get caught up having fun with him and it would have an affect in my world. I found this confusing but wanted to understand it and felt the only way to do that was to live it. On the one hand, no one else could see them and unless they learned how to walk the tree, or move in the astral, it was unlikely they would. So I could not prove to anyone this was really happening to me. This bothered me. I found myself looking for ways to prove this was real to others. They have a great sense of humor and would mess with me constantly actually trying to help me know that it was really happening. See as long as there is doubt then it can cause problems and being that I could not prove it to others it would make me feel like it could be me and my imagination. Then I would be talking to one of them about something very specif Ic and the next day go jump in my car to go to work and a song would come on that was talking about exactly what we had been talking about. I would be listening to the words and feel him watching me and then see him with my third eye. At times I would wake in the morning with a song playing loudly in my head that was different than the one playing on my clock radio that had just come on. I would shake my head and look at my radio thinking that's not right. This happened all the time, still does even if l do not have the radio set or turned on. I will wake up with music playing in my head, hear and feel the familiar buzz or vibration that reminds me of a transporter from Star Trek sealing me back into my body, and open my eyes and realize my radio is not on. Does it make you think of the familiar twilight zone song? I feel that it might be that when I am taken out of body and then sent back, that during the send back tim maybe my astral body is crossing radio waves and that is what I am hearing coming back in. I know I will feel great heat for a moment as if I am being sealed back in my body. Many times I will come conscious in my body and feel as though I have just stepped out of a transporter beam, even to the tingling or buzz feeling. The only thing is the music always seems to fit with something I have been talking about with them, so I tend to think that there may be an answer in the words for me. Another thing was that I was always waking up at 1:11 or 11:11 and sometimes 3:11. Not only that but a timer I have for food, that is not a clock would get set somehow and be moving forward like a clock, and I still do not know how to make it do this. It is also a magnet and is stuck to the hood of my stove so there was no way for this to happen accidentally as it is up high and I only use it when I am cooking on the stove or in the oven. Yet I can not tell you how many times I would go in and find it set to a certain number of hours and minutes. I have never used the hours as I never cook for that long with a timer. When I looked up the numbers in a Kabbalah book they would vaguely point to a question I had asked or a conversation we had. Another thing that happens is on the way back into my body a man will say something to me. During this most recent war between Israel and Palestine, I became lucid in a dream watching a newscast in what seemed to be a small ship with others sitting in seats in front of and beside me. As I strained to hear the newscast, a male came up on my right and says, "This latest one was started by a headless tube." It was such a weird statement that brought totally off the wall pictures into my mind as to what a headless tube was, that I forgot what I had just heard on the newscast. This may have been intended, since I was learning something. Then in the next moment I was coming back into my body and waking up.

I began mentioning these things to others on UFO lists. Mostly because some of the things they were talking about had happened to me and I could relate. I actually thought I had found a group of people I could share with and who could share with me and discuss and figure these things out. Unfortunately some of the people on those lists are counselors who do not believe those having experiences, but think they will be able to help them and do not want anyone else helping what they feel is their delusion along. Then there are those who do believe something is going on and genuinely are looking to figure it out, only their fear will only let them go so far before they too begin saying you can not prove it, meaning so you must be nuts. So they make small comments about how it can not be proved, because the truth, and what that truth implies, begins showing in the relating of it and is scary for them or their ego to acknowledge. It means changing what they have learned from day one in society and that is a big change. If you have read this far in this book you should be able to relate to having a great philosophical discussion and seeming to be figuring something out and suddenly a couple of people who never post, and only lurk in the background of lists, suddenly begin attacking those having the conversation. Usually attempting to get everyone involved looking at some other issue to side track them. Few are aware enough to catch them at it. It is almost always people who do not contribute anything, or those you do not even know showing up from the lurkers isle.

When I began relating on the lists, at first I would get the same feelings that I had when Prometheus had been watching out for me. Fear of me becoming a guinea pig, or of him being caught by the others and then I would begin shaking like I was cold. Then I would get cold to the point I could not type or speak without my teeth chattering. I would stop and sometimes my friends who I had been relating something to would stop me and it would stop after a moment and I could talk again as long as I did not continue speaking about what ever it was he did not want me talking about. A few times I stubbornly would try to continue, only to have it happen again. I finally confronted Chokmah about it and asked why I was being stopped from explaining things to others. I told him I thought they were just what humanity needed now and I could not understand why they were holding me back, and I thought they had a law about stopping our will. I went on about this for days and was not about to give up trying to get them to come forward. I wanted contact. I wanted others to understand what was really happening on earth as I thought it might help with a lot of social issues. That does not mean I want them to take over our lives for us, simply to know the truth so that we would know for sure which direction we should be headed in. How can you make a valid decision when you do not know the truth?

When people begin to understand what is really happening many of the reasons for war are gone, they begin to realize that raising their consciousness is one of the most important things they can do. The answer I received was that it was not my place to do it. I could not understand why since I had known a gray and them and could understand them in ways that it was obvious to me that others could not. Then he told me I already had an important part to play, why would I want another? He made me feel like I wanted to play all the parts, only I did not know what part I was to play or what he was talking about. It was frustrating for me.

Chapter Twelve

Right before Christmas I realized I had not seen Prometheus in the physical for a while like I used to, and I wondered if I would get to see him for Christmas. On Christmas Eve I had gone out for a party and come home early. My son and other roommate were both working late that night and my daughter was gone to a friends to spend the night. I lay down on my couch and turned on the TV and fell asleep. I woke to a clanging like someone opening and closing the fireplace vent and I opened my eyes, sat up and stared at it. It sounded as if someone was coming down the chinmey and I just sat there staring at it. Then I thought they must be coming up the stairs and stopping at the top of the stairs as if listening. I was sitting up by then waiting for which ever person it was to come forward into the firelight from the side of the fireplace where he stood. It almost seemed as though he came out of the side of the fireplace rather than up the stairs, but I had just woke up and logically thought he must have come up the stairs. He seemed to look like my son but even in the dark I could see he had light colored pants on and a light jacket. Although not snowing yet it was cold and these clothes made no sense to me in the dead of winter, and I thought those do not look like the clothes he left in. He heard my thought, looking down at his pants. I said, "Hi", thinking it was my son, and he said, "Hi" and I felt this overwhelming feeling of love and said, "Happy Christmas Eve". He said, "Yeah" and then he pointed as if he had forgotten something in his car and he said, "I have to go." I thought he meant he would be right back after retrieving what ever it was he had left in his car. I smiled and said, "Ok." He ran down the stairs or so it seemed, and at the same time my other room mate came up the stairs from the basement. There was no way they could not have seen each other. As my roommate got up to the top and said, "Hi." I said, "Hi, There is cheesecake in the kitchen I brought home from the party earlier if you want some and when Sherman comes back in tell him also." He looked at me and said, "Is Sherman home?" I looked at him and said, "What do you mean?

Didn't you just pass him on the stairs going out to his car?" He said, "No" and ran down the stairs to look out the front door to see him. Then he came back up and said his car is not there. I stared at him and told him what had just happened and we decided I had just busted them. There was no other explanation for it since if it had been a burglar he would have seen him on the stairs. It was just before midnight by then and I sat thinking about this and that show about the psychic that talks to ghosts was playing. It was the best Christmas present I received that year.

I had already experimented with sex on the astral with other friends and I was attracted to Chokmah, he was so gorgeous I could not keep from looking at him. They are much more open about sex than humans are. To them if you are admiring them it is like saying you are curious, interested in what it would be like with them. When everyone can read each others thoughts, some attitudes change, they have to. I had always felt that everyone should be telepathic while I had Prometheus around because I thought it would force others to be honest. This would be a good thing for humanity. However, I was not attracted to

Prometheus sexually, so this issue was not a problem. I was about to find out just what kind of problem it could be.

Then a message was sent around the internet asking, "Do you want us to come." Many thought this was a hoax, but I knew it was not because I had been hammering them to come forward and although why my wishes come true is sometimes beyond me, many of them do. It was then that I realized someone else had the job of making people aware of them. After all I had been through all my life I was genuinely upset about this because I felt like, what was all this I have gone through for if not this? Then he began coming to me to talk to me on this plane. I would be on the computer and feel him in the room with me. Sometimes he would be standing to my left and watching what I was typing to the list group. I had been trying to quit smoking for at least eight years using both gum, patches and cold turkey, only to resume smoking. I had vacation for two weeks and he asked me if l wanted help quitting smoking. "Of course I would like help!" I exclaimed. "I have been trying to quit for a long time only I do not want to gain a bunch of weight." He nodded. He did that a lot,just nod and smile. It always made me wonder what he had up his sleeve, but I have always liked surprises so I would just smile back and wait and see. After that for the next two weeks, every time I felt like smoking he would come to me and the most deliciously sexual thoughts would bombard my mind and totally make me forget about smoking. In fact I could not get him out of my mind and I was perfectly ok with that. I had never had so much fun with a male, and it was working and I was not smoking and I did not even have the urge to do so. Definitely the way to quit smoking.

Another thing he kept saying to me, "I am not a man." With human males, most are not telepathic enough to pick up on your thoughts except for in the very beginnings of a relationship where you know they are calling or something similar. I could talk to him anytime I wanted, and found myself going to him in his rooms at night. I would leave my body and go up to see him and fall asleep there with him, only to wake up when he sent me back to my body. One day I went up to see him and Osiris was there talking to him. I had met Osiris many years before and greeted him. They are all so beautiful, so perfectly proportioned that I find it hard not to admire them. I can not imagine any human feeling differently. Later he told me I should go see Osiris and talk to him. So I did. I began to get the impression that he wanted me while we were talking and I had heard that they were much less prudish than humans and I was beginning to understand that feeling. Where I was extremely attracted to him, I also loved Chokmah and never was the type of person to keep a string of suitors going. I asked him if we could be friends because I loved talking to him. He always communicated more directly with me, and seemed to have more experience communicating with humans. There are definite differences to their personalities, which I did notice. It was one more thing that convinced me this was not in my imagination.

Osiris was fine with us being friends, so a great friendship began. Meanwhile Chokmah and my relationship was moving right along. My son who was renting a room from me downstairs asked me one day if we could have a dog. His friend had a pit bull puppy that she needed to find a home for. I have never been into dogs much because I like gardens and many dogs dig. I also like my peace and quiet because I meditate, and already had love birds I was trying to find homes for as fast as they multiplied, so said no. Then my son decided he was going to be moving closer to his work. My daughter and I would be left alone then and Chokmah thought I needed more protection. He mentioned as much but then we moved to another topic and it was dropped, or so I thought. One night I heard my son come in at about one thirty in the morning and instead of going back to sleep I went up to visit Chokmah. At three in the morning I had just plopped back into my body, woke up and turned over smiling with that well loved feeling, when I heard a horrible scream right outside my window. There are coyotes that come around and I thought one had attacked one of my cats. I jumped up, donned my robe and slippers and ran outside. It was a puppy that was just there along side my house with no one around and it was scared and crying. Where it came from I never found out. I brought it inside thinking my son had brought it home from his friends anyway and it had gotten out the cat door. So I put it in the bathroom but it began crying, so I brought it upstairs with me. It had huge paws so I thought it was much older than it was. I have an acre and I walked all around it asking neighbors if they had lost a puppy.

No one had lost one. That weekend I took it to the veterinary clinic to have it checked and found out it was 2-3 weeks old. It's paws were about two inches big and they told me one of these days I would not be able to pick him up and put him on the table. They were right so now I am the proud owner of a beautiful Husky-Rottweilder mix at least that is the closest we could come up with. So I received my protection after all and to this day I wonder where he came from.

I was back at work now and the following weekend I went out to trim a thorn tree on the side of my yard. I was doing fine till I got jabbed by the thorn tree and lost my balance dropping the sheers. They landed pointing up, and I had to push off the ladder backwards or land on the sheers. I curled up and expecting to land on my back and have the air knocked out of me, when I felt someone catch me and set me down and I landed with a small plop. I laid there not believing what had just happened since there was no one around but me that I could see. I had felt someone catch me and gently let me go a few inches from the ground rather than from four feet up like I had been. That was enough for the day and I stopped cutting the thorn tree and went inside. The next day I decided to get the rest of it cut. I had shorts on and as I was cutting I felt something land on the back of my leg. Looking around I saw it was a bee. I decided to step down off the ladder with my leg straight and try and blow him off with the wind. It worked but I ended up doing the splits standing up because my other foot was still on the ladder rung and it was a bit higher than I figured. I strained the muscles in my leg so again gave up on the thorn tree. I went in and put witch hazel on my leg and it seemed to help. The following weekend I took the puppy outside to run around and took two steps and collapsed. I had tom the ligaments behind my knee in two different places and taking the two steps running was too much. I was not doing anything for two to three weeks and then only going to work with a walker, it took a good three months to heal to where I could actually walk without limping. I believe my thoughts were to blame on this as I kept wondering if there was someone else in Chokmahs life and if I was intruding. I still did not understand how their relationships worked and was doing my best to understand the different social customs. I rarely if ever saw females at all, and then they did not really talk to me. I kept asking if he could come and see me on my plane and if I would ever be able to see him with my physical eyes. One morning I woke and sat up in bed, only I strangely felt like I was just coming out of a dream and so tried to hold onto it so I would remember it. Then I noticed that my home had windows where there were walls almost like I was on the ship. I walked into the kitchen and there were three small lemon meringue pies on the kitchen counter, then I heard him say he had to leave. I walked towards the hall going back towards the bedroom only to see him outside the windows and running or flying as he went by the windows while my body was back sitting on my bed. He ran so fast he disappeared and reminded me of Mercury with wings on his feet. I was in the most pleasant euphoria all morning. He had actually come to see me, or maybe his ship and my home crossed on our separate dimensions since I did not have the pies when I got up. I felt loved and cared about and was enjoying my time with him immensely. I never did figure out what three lemon meringue pies meant symbolically.

At one point he told me that they were much more open sexually and they found it worked out better for them. When he was gone there were others who would take care of any needs I had and this way he could make sure I was taken care of and watched over while he was away. I asked him how and who would be choosing these guys and he said I would and he would decide if they were acceptable to him. On the one hand I could understand why if they were gone for some time like a sailor they would make arrangements like this, but I was not sure if I would be able to deal with it emotionally. One evening a short time later I went up to see him and he said I should probably go as he was expecting someone important. I said, "Ok I will see you later," and turned to leave and someone caught my hand from behind me and said, "Don't leave on my account." I turned back around and a male had his hand resting on top of mine and yet had hold of me. He was beautiful like the others, perfectly proportioned, and it was fascinating for me that they were all so beautiful. He had long blonde hair and a golden brown colored clothes that looked like soft leather, and he was on fue. I stood there staring at him while the flames seemed to lick at him as if it were his aura almost, but did not burn him. After taking all this in, I noticed his expression did not seem to change and he just watched me rather haughtily as if testing me to see what I would do. I finally said, "Do you realize you are on fire?" He said nothing, still standing there and I was not sure if he understood me from the look on his face. I smiled at him and started to turn my hand over to clasp his and he looked down at it and opened his mouth as if startled and to warn me not to. I felt and saw this rather than heard it and said, "What you can touch me but I can not touch you?" Then out of my peripheral vision I saw Chokmah reach up behind me and I passed out. About twenty minutes later I woke to see him and Chokmah sitting at a table and eating and discussing something seemingly in midair above where I was laying in bed. I lay there and listened, not wanting to move and risk loosing the vision or connection. I could hear him ask Chokmah, "How much does she understand?" and then Chokmah saying, "She's awake and can hear us." I could too. Sometimes I would wake and think about him and suddenly would be watching him with my minds eye, not really eave dropping or not intending to but more like just before you fall asleep but before you begin dreaming and you hear something and are straining to understand what you are hearing. I began to wonder if l was living two lives at the same time. One with them and one here, and did not care. All I knew was that I felt at home with them and loved them all. He gave me a dress to wear that was a beautiful dark green color that wrapped around me but was very full. It is still amazing to me. I asked him if there were other races that they dealt with that were here around earth, and one night I had a lucid dream about meeting a guy who looked very much like Matt Damon only he was on a ship and had desert storm colored camouflage type of uniform on. He did not talk too much but showed me around his ship and quarters because I made a comment that it must be cramped on long trips. Then he took me and introduced me to a orange haired woman that ran his store on board and I was wearing the same green dress I had been given. I was told her name but can not remember it now. Her hair was cut similar to a Dutch boy hair style only it was orange, not red or auburn and she was about four and a half feet tall. She showed me the store, and I commented that there was not much in it and asked if they needed provisions. She looked around and said they would be getting more in a week or so. There were blankets and gear and clothes all in beige, gold, khaki green, and a deep red color. It reminded me of a commissary store. Then I woke at home. I am still amazed at how I get answers to my questions. A few days later I had a lucid dream, where when I woke in the dream I was in front of a house and there were two picnic tables there. I was sitting at one with my daughter and another girl and we were waiting for the aliens to come so we could meet them. After a minute there was almost a parade with two guys in front that had white tight pants to the knees on, with jackets and lacy cuffs.

They had long blonde curly hair and really white faces and red mouths. I only got a glimpse of them before they turned away and hid their faces. Then there was one of the orange haired girls walking a baby buggy only the baby talked like a grownup. There were a few different kinds of humanoid beings, some brown or blue, some shorter and then I saw what appeared to be a satyr who was trying to keep all of them together. I noticed that the guys with the white faces had gone in the house and said something to the orange haired girl about it. She said that they knew how their faces affected humans and so had gone in the house so they could watch without scaring us. I felt horrible at that. I decided to go try and talk to them in the house. I am usually not scared so easily, and I did not want them to miss out on meeting us because of human prejudices. I went over to the house and there was another big alien there like a faerie who told me I might not want to go in there. I told him it was ok, that they could stay in the shadows if they wanted, but it was not fair for them to miss out. He let me go in and the others inside stepped behind a pillar and into the shadows. I could feel their fear that I would get scared and then one stepped out and stood there and I just stood there looking down and said to them I did not feel it was fair that they missed out so I came in to see if they wanted to talk. I began to look up and he darted back in the shadows and I woke up. What a dream, or was it? It is hard to tell in lucid dreams sometimes but in all honesty I have begun to think of them as real. Like in this one, I was talking to the same girl I saw on board the ship a few nights before in another apparent lucid dream. I can also remember seeing those guys with the white faces and stretched out red mouths at some time in the past. They almost look like a mime in a King Louis costume of satin brocade only when they turn their face towards you their mouth is bright red and stretched kind of ghoulishly so it gives them a rather frightening appearance. Maybe they are part of the faerie world, I am not sure. Even if the faerie world were different beings from humans, I feel they were once living with us on top of earth until humanity began thinking they were better than other living creatures. At one point I realized that what seemed to me to be causing the most trouble amongst humanity was a belief that because they had God's grace or were the chosen ones,

it meant they were better than the rest of the animals.

That God meant for them to conquer and rule the world

rather than manage it. This is the egos thinking, trying to

prove it is as good or better than daddy. The brain or Borg

of humanity. Then the prejudices began and they have

continued until this day even among our own kind. It was

then that the gods thought that at that stage in humanities

development it might be better if they just faded into the

background where most of humanity could not see them. A

half dimension away. Close enough to monitor us and our

progress and yet far enough away for the jealousies to not

have an effect. If humanities egos were not trying to prove

themselves like the gods, then maybe they would learn to

get along with others.

My daughter had an older friend come to stay with

us for a few nights and she wanted to go out one evening

during the week. I did not allow her to go out during the

week because of school, but she had learned that I could

not really make her stay home because of the laws. She

was giving me a bad time about it when Osiris finally said,

"Would you like some help?" Well I was not sure what help entailed and said, "As long as she is not hurt, I would love some help." Her friend was sitting there on our couch and had been around me long enough to know what my grins meant, and asked me what I had done. I told her I was just offered help and took them up on it. About that time my daughter screamed. Her friend and I looked at each other and then ran back to her. She had been running back and forth from her room to the bathroom putting on makeup and spraying her hair. She had run back into her room to finish getting ready and then ran back into the bathroom and grabbed the hair spray and actually touched what was clinging to the nozzle. It was a gray spider about two inches big. It's tail was about an inch long and looked like gray silk and it was clinging to the button. It was out of this world looking. I have never seen a spider that looked like this. It almost looked like it had claws like a crab. I flushed it down the toilet, laughing and her friend is staring at me with her eyes wide open. I then looked at my daughter and said, "That is what you get for being smart mouthed with me." I could not figure out how it got on top of the hairspray like someone had placed it there, when she had just been in there seconds before. I had never seen anything that even remotely looked like it, and I looked on the internet for a while the next day trying to find it but could not. Osiris and I became great friends after that. That had been the perfect thing to do and I loved him for it. I was not sure how he did it but that did not matter to me. I love magic and always have so I felt being around them I could only learn and that is what I felt life was about. I asked all of them who I was that all these things happened to me and that I knew them. I would get answers from them as thoughts, but they were too fantastic to believe and I would again think I was ego tripping.

As I said, all of them were always trying to help me see this was real and not in my imagination. After seeing crop circles I asked them about them and was told they were in fact done by them on many occasions. So I asked him if he could do one for me so I would have proof of them. Something like a heart maybe. That was when the first one with a heart in it, at least that I had seen, showed up. Of course no one would believed me as usual, but I thought it was sweet anyway. Then I made mention that I never got to see ships when all these people all over saw them. Shortly after that I was sitting at the computer one afternoon and just happened to have my camera sitting there when he nudged me mentally and said come out side. So I did with my camera. There was an orb right there in front of me. I went in and got my daughter and told her to come look and she saw it too. I still have pictures of it. So you see in many ways they were showing me, "this is real," and making it fun at the same time. They have a great sense of humor.

Chapter Thirteen

One day I went up to see Chokmah, who until then I thought was Jehovah, and had actually began calling him Jah. Upon my arriving he said he was about to leave and go see his parents. I asked him if I could come, out of the blue, mostly out of pure curiosity and he said, "Sure I don't see why not." I had not expected that, but I thought cool. Suddenly he was bowing in front of me towards my right and he was on a red carpet and we had not moved. I looked to my right and there was a beautiful young female with honey colored hair that was twisted back and up, and then hanging on her right side in relaxed curls. She wore what looked like a Greek toga. She met my eyes for just a moment and then turned her head, telepathically speaking towards her left, and as I followed her gaze, here stood a male king also in a white toga who was studying me very intently. This really caught me off guard and I looked back at Chokmah who was still kneeling with head down in front of them, who had darker long hair and looked more Annunaki with tanner skin and the Egyptian looking pleated skirt. This male king was beautiful with a square jaw, deep blue eyes like Osiris' that were just slightly bigger than ours, and shorter curly blonde hair like an angel. In fact he was one of the first I had seen with shorter hair. He stood there the whole time staring at me, watching my every thought run across my face. The female for her part was telling him my every thought or maybe her interpretation of my thoughts since I am sure he could read my thoughts also. As I stood there taking this all in, I looked down at Chokmah and said, "Should I be bowing?" He glanced up and said, "No, it is not necessary," and looked back down. I looked back at his parents wondering who they were, and heard the male telepathically say, "Jupiter." I do not think I will ever forget that moment. The gods, I was meeting one of the gods. The look in his eyes is ancient and yet his face looks almost boyish it looks so young. I found this amazing, and then thought this must be Hera. I thought how she did not look at all like I expected her to look, and she looked back over her shoulder as if stif ling a laugh and I felt like she said, "She thinks I am her." Then I understood she was Pallas Athena his daughter who is ever with him. Then the thought entered my mind of Zeus and his playing around with all the women and I looked up at him only to find his intense eyes looking through me. I thought, "No, he wouldn't", and looked down at Chokmah thinking, it was his son, and then I was back sitting on my couch. As I sat there thinking about this, I realized how flattered I was to have his attention. I was really confused now, me, who had always been a one man woman found myself in the situation of loving them all and I did not know what to think about it, or how I would ever be able to choose. Well I thought they had started this and they would just have to live with it. I could understand now the rumors I had heard about some alien beings having much more open sexual relationships and thinking humanity was rather prudish and closed. This was just the beginning of a wonderful affair with all of them where I would learn different things from each one. Zeus came to see me that night and I asked him who I was and what Chokmah's real name was? He told me he could not tell me Chokmah's name and that he would have to tell me that himself. "As for you," he said, "you are my wife." I sat there stunned for a moment and asked, "How can I be your wife?" "That is just too unbelievable, I would be magical." Even as I said it, all of the things I had done and seen ran through my mind and I had to pause and think it through. He did look really familiar to me and more I felt like I knew him deep down. This was just such an egotistical thought I could not deal with it and decided to change the subject. "I do not remember Pallas having a child," I stated to him. He watched me a lot, and his eyes are such an intense blue and seemed to know everything. Zeus always gives me an answer and that is one thing that really endears him to me. He seems to understand the way I think better in some ways. Where Chokmah would answer me and sometimes take a long period of time and move through my life so that I understood and felt his answer clearly, Zeus would answer me telepathically and very matter of fact. When I got upset with Chokmah about seeming to pass me around to others, Zeus pointed out to me that it was not his fault.

He thought I wanted to be with these others, and at the same time as he said this I received a mental picture of me thinking about them. I looked at him aghast. "You mean every time I think of one of you trying to figure something out to myself, he thinks I want to be with you and so arranges it?" That sure turned the tables on me. Even though I was probably a little more used to telepathically speaking with others, there were still times when I would allow thoughts to run through my mind and not even realize I was doing it, or where they came from. Most humans do and do not realize that many times those thoughts are not their own. The fact is we pick up on others thoughts all the time and many times think they are our own thoughts and act on them. When someone asks you later why did you do that, they do not know. During the 70's the phrase, "The devil made me do it" or, "My evil twin took over", became popular, but still not many really believed what they were saying when they gave that excuse. They simply did not realize how close they were to the truth. Not that a devil did it, but that some one else had observed the situation and thought the thought, and they had heard it mentally and acted on it thinking it was theirs. Many times I would hear thoughts and take a back seat to them by just allowing them to pass through, while considering them. Even now I wonder how many who are reading this will think of someone they think is handsome and wonder what it would be like to be with them, knowing that you would not act on the thought. It is quite normal to ponder other people and the way they live, the way they dress, or the way they look, just trying to understand them with nothing sexual meant by it. When telepathy is a fact of life those thoughts will have to be watched and I was getting a first hand lesson why, and also why they were much more sexual than us. From what I have seen they are all beautiful. All different, but proportionally perfect and because of it are beautiful. I have found that amazing and so would really look at them taking in all the details and wondering how they could all be so beautiful and yet look different? To find out that my thoughts had been misconstrued by Chokmah made me feel bad. Zeus took all of this in and told me to go talk to him. I walked away and then I felt bad, thinking I had just turned him down. It was a very confusing time for me. I went back up to let Zeus know how I felt and he said, "You think I will be lonely because you are elsewhere?" He waved his arm and I followed it as he said, "How could I be lonely with so many around?" There before me was a spiral with angels all along the sides going down into it, and he and Pallas were standing up at the top on what seemed like a ledge overseeing it all. This was seventh heaven. I felt really small seeing all this, and felt like my company meant nothing to him. How could it when he could be with anyone he wanted any time. I left then feeling quite dejected. I could see his face behind me realizing he had hurt my feelings, and then I realized some of why Zeus and Hera had fought so. He was air, mind, all mental and intellectual where Hera was emotional and empathic. I wanted to go see Chokmah but after that experience felt like my thoughts should be my own for a while and went instead to my place on the astral to think and be alone. I knew Zeus had not meant to hurt my feelings or make me feel like nothing, but somehow knowing that did not help. It seemed to me that their way of relationships, where it may be more open, seemed less emotional and more mental. They were spirits, angels not humans and this is what Chokmah had meant when he kept saying to me, "I am not a man." I needed to figure out who I was and what I was doing here. Osiris came up and asked to join me and I was grateful for his company. He was always so kind, thoughtful and compassionate. I knew from our first meeting that he was very powerful, but he would always try to help me with my confusion. He knew I was trying very hard to understand their ways, and I always enjoyed our times together. I felt like I was having a hard time with the relationship part of our friendships because I did not really know my place. I had never felt at home on Earth and had never been happier than when I was with them, but was still confused. I had set up my own moral thoughts on relationships and sex as a teenager on Earth that allowed me to feel honorable about myself within Earth's society, and now they were not working. With humans, most people stick to one person or society begins to think of them as loose. Yet in the gods society marriage seemed to be for the lineage and sex was a very natural creative and loving act between them, even between family members. I did not understand this and Osiris pointed out to me that Zeus's son was also my son. That got me. It took me some time after that to go back and see him. It was not until I realized much later that all of these spirits had been incarnating into bodies on Earth for thousands of years trying to help humanity to evolve into a new being. During different lives they frequently would end up with mothers, brothers, sisters, and fathers as mates since they would be drawn to them from deep memories of previous lives while in a new body. Of course not until we remember our past lives do we realize this, but it happens anyway. This also shows up in astrology charts. Still knowing this and dealing with it on a personal level is two different things and I was very confused.

Rama had told his students once, being confused is a great place to be, because then you were open to change and learning was easier.

Osiris and I had something in common. We both loved gardens. So I asked him if we could go walking in his garden some day. At the time I thought his garden must really be beautiful and I genuinely wanted to see it. Unfortunately as sometimes happens when I am around them, my consciousness passed out and I only woke up when he was walking me back home. Even so I did see this beautiful twilight realm and a tropical looking garden right before we crossed under a limb and I recognized my own yard. He stopped and said that was as far as he could come and I would have to go the rest of the way by myself. I hugged him tight and gave him a kiss on his cheek I was so happy he had actually taken me for a walk in his garden. He did not have to after all. A few weeks later I could see him in my minds eye outside my home and there was another guy with him walking towards the back yard. I asked who he was and he said, "Oh he's just another who wants to know about love." I watched him walk towards my backyard with what looked like a hatchet over his shoulder, and pondered why he had brought him to me. I would learn the answer to this later, but it was at this time just another hint. We would have some nice conversations together. By then I knew they were shape shifters and so was always asking them if the form I was seeing was their real form or just one that they thought I would be comfortable with. To this questioning they were wary as they did not want to freak me out. But I wanted to know who I was talking to for sure and so finally convinced my woodman giant to show me another form he took. When a spirit has evolved enough on their own they get to a point that they are allowed to incarnate into a human body with a soul. I gathered that my woodman friend was just getting curious about it and was observing me to help him decide if he wanted to go that route or not. I learned from him that he was the same being whether he was in his humanoid form or in one of his animal forms. He felt the same empathically to me. I felt secure knowing he was around even if he was not on this plane, I knew he was there. Since he wanted to know about love I showed him love and asked him for a kiss one day. A few nights later I woke in a lucid dream and sat up in bed, with Zeus on my right and some others standing around at the foot of my bed. I was puzzled at first as I did not understand what was up. I looked at Zeus and he nodded to someone on the left of me. I looked over to see my friend the woodsman walk over and lay on top of me fully clothed and give me a kiss. I was so surprised he had actually kissed me, it woke me up. I sat in my bed laughing and giggling for a few minutes thinking how sweet that had been. I have not seen him since then and can only hope he has found happiness. He asked me to draw his picture and I did .

They all have asked me to draw them, and I never really felt I was a great artist so was afraid I would not be able to do them justice. They are all so beautiful, each different and yet each proportionally perfect. I am still working on Pallas and Thoth at this time. Pallas asked me when I went up to see Zeus and she was there. I do not see many females so asked her what she thought about the golden statue of her in Tennessee I had just seen on the internet. I do not think it does her justice, as she has a pure clean beauty and that statue is too gold and gaudy and she is anything but gaudy. It was then that she asked me to draw her so she could see what I thought she looked like. Pallas to me looks like the girl next door, only there is an elegance to her that shows good breeding.

Another time out of complete curiosity I went to Osiris and asked him what was this stuff about weighing the heart against a feather? I felt a heart would always weigh more than a feather, so what was the deal. It seemed kind of a set up to me. Then we had long conversations and he asked me about my life. He asked me what were the worse things I thought I had done and I told him. Then he said, "That he did not think those were that bad and had understood exactly why I had done them," then he hugged me and I suddenly felt so light I felt like I was floating. I understood then that what he had just done for me, was the basis of confession in churches, only somehow I doubted that people left feeling as good as I felt then. He was glowing golden and I was glowing with love for this being that was so full of love, kindness and compassion. He is truly amazing not only to look at but to talk to and I positively adore him.

Chapter Fourteen

I have noticed on more than one occasion that the spirits react rather strangely to me telling them I love them. Not all of them, but some. I did not say anything but pondered it to myself. Mistake, for there is no, "to yourself," when everyone is telepathic. I finally asked Osiris if there were such a thing as a demon. I asked because I was genuinely wondering by then if demons were only something superstitious humans who feared any being that was different than themselves, like shape shifters or if there really were such a thing. He asked me what is the difference between a spirit and a demon. He never gives me the answers outright, rather he will ask me questions that lead me to the answer. A spirit has a soul in limbo that he will go on teaching at some point and a demon has lost his soul for what he taught it, is what I said guessing. The thing is that when someone dies the spirit gets separated from the soul for the interim until they are reborn into a body again. When I told some of my friends there I loved them, they would get this look on their faces like they did not know what to say, or they did not want to hear that. I finally asked one saying, "You do not want to hear that do you?" He showed me a necklace of silver that looked like two clasped hands from the wrists down. All the fingers were touching so they looked like a cage only there was nothing in the cage. I took this to mean his heart (soul) was elsewhere so he had no feelings for the moment. This gave me further confirmation that my understanding of spirits and souls was close but not exact yet.

Osiris had now confirmed what Zeus had said, so during the day while I was at work and could not really go see them I would think on this. About a six months before Rama left, we were talking up on the astral one day and I asked him again why it was that I could do all the things I had done. Earlier in the day I had been working and studying and had realized that the whore of Babylon was not a city or state like they wanted us to think, but the soul of the Earth. Then when I was talking to him about it, I read his mind and repeated what I had picked up to him.

He quickly stopped me from voicing it and said, "Don't even think it," as if someone else would hear my thoughts and find me.

I was shown what and who I was over and over, but felt it was too egotistical to believe, so would put it aside and keep searching. Over and over, I came to the same conclusions in differing ways. Always I felt like when you hear someone say they were King Henry in their last life. I would think, "Yeah right," and keep looking. I always felt everyone wants to be someone famous but most of us were just an ordinary person. The only problem was I kept running into the same wall so to speak. I began sharing what I had learned within philosophy, UFO's, and the occult on the internet. I felt like I could share what I knew and help others with some pieces of information that I figured out, and they in turn could help me with information they had figured out. This did help because I then found information that I had not had previously. I had to pick out the truths from the different articles, so that one would give me a bit, and then another would give me a different bit. Eventually a whole picture began to emerge, that again led me to the same answer.

For the first time in my life, and I found this strange that I had never come across it before, I was shown an article by Jack Parsons. He looked so familiar to me. When I read his letters, I found one that could have been me talking to myself. It was suppose to be him channeling the goddess talking to her incarnated self, and I got the chills again. He had done much of this down by where I first had been abducted in the Mohave Desert. The Goddess that had appeared to him had red hair and green eyes and had told him she would be come into life, reincarnate within 7 years from 1949. I was born in 1954 = 19 = to manifest= eve= Teth = Leo, on August 3rd, 8=3. Love= Understanding. See what I mean... I am a Leo and my sun is at 11 degrees, my moon is at 11degrees Libra and my rising sign is 7 degrees Capricorn. My numbers really are 7/11. Magic. According to Jones 7 degrees Capricorn is an Avatar not to mention all my planets are between 16 Cancer and 4 Scorpio, (my 7th, 8th, and 9th with the MC being Scorpio) except for Mars in the 12th in Sagittarius. Libra is strong in my chart which is why he called her to Earth, to work on the relationships and help change what mankind thought. He felt love was the only thing that could save humanity from themselves. Then there was February 28th the day they did the rite, the day is very important to me also. Still when confronted by all this most people would say coincidence, but I do not believe in coincidences anymore, I have seen too much to tell me otherwise. Where I can not be positive, the faerie that I saw in the desert as a child and the one I saw in the creek when I was older looked very much like Mr. Parsons only with long hair. I just could not help but think if l was this being then I would have many more powers than I do. Where it is true it would explain many things I have been able to do, I felt surely others had some of these abilities too.

Then there was Zeus whom I adored from the moment I saw him. So I questioned this being his wife and went at the question from that direction. I asked him how I could be his wife if I was having relationships with others and he explained to me how their relationships were different than humans. Their marriages were for breeding purposes as well as love but they saw sex as a natural outgrowth of love and were not so prudish as humans. Only Hera according to mythology had been jealous. I began to realize that as a spirit being with many others was natural to them. Then I asked him what all the stories about jealousy was about and why was there such a problem. This answer took me a little longer to get, but some months later I was to understand that because during the lifetime as Nephthys, after what had happened between Set and Osiris, Hera who was a reincarnation of Nephthys, had felt bad. She was determined when she got together with Zeus to keep her vows. Zeus for his part had been told that his heir would overthrow him(the ego) and had swallowed Meris the Titan whole and then gone on to bear Pallas when Hades(Osiris) cut his head open. Pallas was born or manifested a fully developed thought form "from and on the astral plane." This could happen because Meris is still with Zeus within him. So Zeus is not just what you could say is a normal spirit, for he is more. He has emotions and does show them. At one point after I had met him I thought I had figured everything out and was trying to figure a way out of this silly situation on Earth and had him playing the bad guy. He showed such emotion saying, "I do not want be seen as the bad guy," that I looked at him and fell in love with him all over again. I felt his emotions and realized how silly I was being. None of them should have to play the bad guy, for none of them are. What he is, is a merging of the female Titan soul and male spirit. Which is also humanities destiny if we merge our spirit and soul, because our souls come from the Titan, Tiamat, Gaia, Hera the Earth. So this is why I say that those who are destroying the Earth on purpose will loose their souls, they are destroying them. Men relate more to the spirit which is why religions tended to follow the spirit in our world. However the females tend to relate more to the soul and its emotional being within us all. This is why when our energy starts to raise, men fall in love with a female they think of as the goddess and will say things like they have never felt so loved, and why females when their energy begins to raise they meet up with their male spirit that knows exactly what the soul loves and imagines and gives it to her. The telepathic connection is of the spirit and the empathic connection is of the soul. Another thing I might point out here is why the human males find it easier to raise their energies than women. So much so it was thought women could not raise their energies and so were not taught for a long time under Eastern religions.

Even now most of their instructions are written with the male in mind. Since the males related more to the masculine spirits it is easier for them to raise their energy. The souls persona being male in this case relates with the ego and spirit in an intellectual way. The soul can understand the spirit in an empathic way and transfer this into an intellectual understanding better than the spirit can understand the souls emotions. When a female and female persona, the male spirit contributing the ego has a more difficult time relating to the emotional demands of the soul and what it wants, so trust is harder to come by. Excess emotionalism creates chaos in the brain to the spirit, where excess intellectualism of the emotions creates lack of desire to create by the soul. Which by the way is one of the problems with the grays. I spent hours talking to Prometheus about emotions and controlling mine. See when we get upset it affects them: they do not know what to do they just want the chaos to stop. See people are very honest when they cry and their thoughts let their spirits know exactly what they need to make it better. I finally pointed out to him that when you control your emotions to that extent you tend to stop desire.

Desire comes from emotions, and so does imagination, but when you stop desire you stop propagating and go extinct. What they need to do is not control their emotions which is really limiting themselves, but balance them with intellect. It is really all about merging into a new being in the hierarchy but with equality of emotion(soul) and mind(spirit), spirits with souls like what Zeus and Thoth are. This is one relationship that will use all your relationship skills you have learned between human relationships and you will not be able to cheat on without cheating yourself.

I was also shown how He-ra (literally the earth), and Nephthys(lady of the house) and Gaia among others were all the same being. Just like Zeus, Jupiter, Jehovah, El, Al among others were all the same being. Hearing of people not being able to get a name out of some alien beings they were conversing with began to make sense. To a spirit, a label like a name is restricting. After all air, does not like to be restricted even in relationships. As they evolve or change, their names change also to suit the new idea or thought that they are. While I am on the subject of spirits, I have to say that I view them as another race of beings and even though only people who have raised their energy levels actually see them, this does not mean they are simple ghosts. One day I went up to the astral to see Zeus and he showed up with the head of a hawk.

He asked me if this bothered me and I laughed and said only if you try to kiss me as I can not quite see how I would kiss a hawk. Even when he is in humanoid form he has huge white wings, so large in fact at one point I thought they were his bed. They are shape shifters and can change into any shape they want. In April of 2006 I hired a couple of guys to help me with my yard. I rarely do this and my yard is almost always a peaceful habitat where animals can come. As one of the men went to the back to begin weed whacking in the enclosed garden area getting ready to turn the soil I ran in the house to grab some gloves. I came out a different door in the back in ttime to see the man working away weed whacking and ten feet above him was a huge golden looking hawk circling and watching him. He circled him once more and then looked up and saw me standing there watching him. He flew right towards me with his mouth open and called to me and to this day I swear he cocked his head and smiled at me before flying over the top of my house. I was very touched by this, how could I not be. Then a couple of days later I asked the man if he had seen the hawk while he was working. He said, "Hawk?" I whistled like a hawk and the hawk answered me. I smiled at the man and did it again, and he answered me again. He was surprised and said, "He is answering you."

About a week later I was digging in the dirt and getting rid of the grass stubs and planting and it was hot. I had my head down and would not even have noticed the hawk but he flew over my head and called to me. I stood up and waved and called back to him, as swooping around him he flew off back towards his nest. This relationship went on for the whole time he had his nest, then one day I had my door on the deck open and heard him call. I ran out to wave and he and his female hawk and two new babies on their maiden flight with their white tail feathers spread wide flew over. I felt completely honored to see this. I told Zeus I thought that was the sweetest thing I had ever seen, and he said, "So you like my hawk <u>hmmm</u>?" I have always loved big birds. The anima-al is very beautiful and smart and also explains why people see anima-als do strange things sometimes. Do I think all animals are the anima of gods, no but they could be at any time which is another reason not to eat meat above a certain level of evolution. Which I do not know about the rest of you but it makes me wonder if the stories in Enoch were based on eating of "animals" by the children of spirits, us, and eating of the spirit, see?

The next time I asked Chokmah who I was I received a strange answer. I guess I had asked so many times he thought I was actually asking who I was in my prior life. Occasionally I would still find my clocks and timers set to 1:11 or wake feeling like I had just been dumped into my body and look at my clock to set to 11:11 or 1:11. This time I got up the next morning and decided I would make a coffee cake. When I reached for the timer it said, 13:22.

As I watched though it changed to 13:23. This stunned

me as it is a timer and not a clock. I do not know how to

make it go forwards. I began looking this up in my books

on Kabbalah and only found a reference to, Lily of the

Valley on 1321. It was only divisible by 2 to 661 which

made reference to Esther and a name for a rose in Latin.

It was while I was doing a search for this Latin name

that I found a reference to Vagabond, and this is how

following serendipity works. Some will think this is nuts

she could have found any word, and this is true, but I did

not just find any word, I came across another word that

"meant" something to "me." This word had always caught

my attention, to the point that one day in a used book

store many years before, I had bought a poetry book by

this name. When I got it home and had a chance to go

through it I found nothing. It was as though it was only

the name of the book that had caught my eye, but the

contents were meaningless to me. When I looked up the

link to Vagabond I found information about another

author. Colette a French writer who had written a book

called Vagabond, and strangely had died the day I was

born. This gave me chills, which always had told me I was on the right track. I began looking up articles on her and found we were very much alike in many ways. She loved to garden and even in her last days had to be by a window where she could watch the garden. She loved herbalogy, and had once set up her home during the war to help the Foreign Legion guys coming back from the war that she received an honorary medal for, the only woman ever to receive it. Where I love herbs and have helped many people with my knowledge of them, I have always stated emphatically that I could not be a nurse or healer as it would tear me up emotionally. I now think I know why. I always had a strange affinity for the Foreign Legion also and could never figure out why. She loved to dance and in fact danced at Moulon Rouge.

Just the name Moulon Rouge has always called to my soul and I love to dance and have done it for exercise all my life and took belly dancing, twice, and disco dancing while I was four months pregnant to keep in shape. When the movie Moulon Rouge came out I went to see it and bought the DVD. I also took four years of

French in school because I at the time I felt I had lived there in another life and wanted to go visit someday, and even told my French teacher that when she asked my why I had chosen French as a second language. I also picked up the accent quickly. Colette's independence due it would seem, to her first disastrous marriage to an older man and subsequent marriages taught her to do for herself. I am very independent and it has caused me problems in relationships also. The more I read about her the more I believed I was her in this past life. Almost everything about her was a continuation in my life, slightly changed with growth but obviously a continuation. Even to writing. All my life I have wanted to write a book. Now not only do I know why, but why it took so long to do it. Her writing was about everyday life for her, where she would bare her emotions and feelings before the world only using another character to play her or the people she was speaking of. She was empathic. She wrote 50 books and now that I am 51, I find myself writing the novel I always wanted to write about "my life as me", in very much the same way she would have written it. I am still amazed at this. Gigi, the movie with Kathryn Hepburn and Maurice Chevalier was her novel. She worked closely with Kathryn on this. I have always loved Kathryn Hepburn and genuinely felt like I knew her. So many things make sense to me about my feelings about odd things now. Even why I have been doing accounting and bookkeeping work for 35 years, she never felt she was good with money. I find it hard to put to words my amazement at this, but it did not stop there. I was being given answers and as soon as I was at ease with it, was shown more.

The day after I learned this, I was in such a state of awe when I woke the next morning. I made coffee and walked out on the deck to look at the garden and drink it. It was a beautiful morning and one of my cats came up on railing on the deck next to me. Suddenly from across the yard a huge bird came flying towards us. It did not stop until it was three feet in front of me off the deck, with my cat looking at it with that come a little closer look drooling at the bit. It was a huge ring neck dove and it fluttered there in front of me long enough to recognize the ring around it's neck and say, "Well hello." Then it took off towards the south of the yard. With that I sat down and picked my jaw up off the ground. I mean you can only shake your head in disbelief so much you know, sooner or later you have to start believing these things are happening to you for a reason, even if it does sound egotistical. I think that has been the biggest stumbling block for me. I have tried so hard not to be egotistical all my life that even though I was told over and over again why these things were happening to me from many different directions and beings, I just could not bring myself to belief it. Sooner or later though there are not any other answers and then the most wonderful thing happens. As soon as you begin believing, all the answers to all your questions start coming from every direction imaginable.

When Zeus told me some time back that they were the egos, I was confused. To me the egos are the cause of all the pain in the world and I could not reconcile the egos with these wonderful beings I was with. It has taken me a couple of years to get this answer from him and little by little he has shown me how they are the egos. The spirits create the ego to communicate with the soul, as a translator, and a receptor of their thoughts. As they are not in the body with the soul, who is still waking up, their ego begins to believe it has all the answers, and it is the god. They have lost the control to their own ego, their own creation within the third dimension has now convinced the personality that it is the higher self. I believe this happens because the spirit is not actually in the body with us at all times, only the soul. Just like the old stories about the Sun and the Moon, where the Moon diminishes herself within the shells(body). The spirit is outside the body and that is who caught me when I fell off the ladder. The proof of this is there for all who have been saved by an angel. Some think of this as their guardian angel. I say it is your spirit, your angel, and it does not have to be within your body with you for it has the ego that translates between the spirit and the soul within the body.

More and more began coming back to me, little by little. They all helped reminding me of previous lives with them and who they were. The seven headed beast that Babalon rides are the egos but also the original seven spirits. She is riding without reins or that she has gained

control of by balancing herself with them. You could think
of them as the tests we must all balance to evolve. Each of
the original seven gave us a test of positive and negative
to learn to balance. I believe that the way most have been
taught about the seven deadly sins is in error. They are
told to avoid them completely and strive for the opposite
virtues. The only problem with this is the opposite of
laziness is diligence, where it is true laziness is a sin, so is
over working for others so that they do nothing. For then
in leaving nothing for them to do you are helping them to
hurt themselves and making a slave out of yourself. I can
see where gluttony is very bad both for the temple(your
body) and for others who do not have enough to eat, but
abstinence is surely just as bad. Starving the body (the
temple) is just as bad on the body and we have witnessed
this in many young girls trying to stay skinny so that their
body(car) looks good but their soul pays for it. Greed is
terrible and this world has a major problem with it, but
many do not see the fallacy that liberality can do great
harm too in not teaching responsibility to those you
give everything away to. How many poor little rich kids

have you heard of who thought they were above the laws.

Envy I think should be changed to begrudge for it better

describes the sin of not being happy for someone else's

good fortune and yet I think we have all at one time or

other known someone who was so kind of spirit they

refused to see how others were taking advantage of them,

and let others harm them, and by doing so allowed them

to harm themselves. Anger it seems to me has gotten

a very bad rap to the point where counselors have held

classes where people are allowed to get angry, so patience

has definitely been done to death during this time. What

is more holding anger in only makes it leak out in your

imagination where we create our world. There is a point of

time where patience turns into fear of failure if you should

choose the wrong path and thus not choose at all. Lust I

believe has been twisted also by those who had to have it

all or nothing for surely chastity is just as bad as starving

the body as many have found out. Excessive pride should

speak for itself and yet if it is taken to mean pride against

God's grace, then the unmerited divine assistance given

to mankind for their sanctif Ication has indeed caused

the pride itself, that mankind can destroy and pollute the Earth shows no humility what so ever. Throwing out the Ten Commandments from the schools and courts of law also ring high on this sin as does feeling we can protect ourselves against alien intruders without God's help.

Yet to be so humble as to not question anything is as great a sin against the soul as it is against God, for even God learns from us as we learn from God. There has to be balance in all, MAAT. So in truth the whore of Babalon is not a evil person for she is balancing them all for everyone to see as an example of the MAAT. In the stories it is the antichrist that kills her. The anti-christed (christed being a person who's energies have merged in the hermetic marriage, or is enlightened), =1would be the ego that fears death, knowing it will not continue in it's present state. Fear of change. I think it is general knowledge now that the ego causes most of the problems on earth so I have not said anything new here. It is my belief that the ego is created by the spirit when it incarnates into this dual world and the persona is created by the soul. The spirit, being the mind knows all and it is because of this that the ego thinks it is in control, but it is only the mask of the spirit so that it may communicate with others in this world,just as the personality is the mask of the soul. The spirit gives to the soul and teaches it, it is there when the soul needs it. Just like if the personality gets it's feelings hurt the ego comes out to defend it. It is here that the personality and ego take on a life of their own and think "they are the real beings" because in the beginnings of our life we are still under the veil of forgetfulness and do not realize what we really are. Even the masters who have come in to help others evolve, have the same thing happen and must strive to know their higher selves. We are all dual beings until we merge in the hermetical marriage, or alchemical marriage and become enlightened in the process. The only way this happens is if your soul and spirit accept each other and trust each other as equals, and for each person this will take different lessons and knowledge, but the process is basically the same. Meditation though is the key to opening the gate.

Chapter Fifteen

At the end of July 2006 or the beginning of August I had a lucid dream about the underworld. I had noticed many times if I told any of my new friends I loved them that they acted like they did not know what to say. I began to feel like they did not want to hear me say it. This lucid dream I think was in answer to this feeling that I had not voiced to any of them. Just goes to tell you what happens when everyone can read your mind. I became conscious on a cobblestone street and a small girl ran up to me and grabbed my hand. She said she wanted to help me but was being held back by someone I did not quite hear who. She said she would take me and show me where he was. There was a huge old mansion on top of a hill with rot iron fencing around it. As I looked at this place I could see a guy peeking around corners and around curtains at us. He would never come out and face me though. Finally I decided we should leave since he would not come out. We turned around and began to walk down the cobbles and there on the walkway was my rose wood box that I keep my Tarot cards in. I had to search for one for that deck because of the strange size of the cards. My box is all inlaid woods of different kind but on top it is smooth and red colored like Mahogany. Only as I picked it up I noticed it had been carved in the middle in very ornate lettering with a border around it, and it said, "The Rad." It was beautiful. We left there and I walked down to a house that I thought was mine and walked in. There was a red velvet sofa against the wall with a coffee table in front of it. Between the table and the sofa on the floor were a bunch of papers as if they had just been on the table and had been pushed on the floor so the table could be used. I took this in and then looked up to see a man about 6 foot tall just standing there acting shy. He had a hat on and on one side I could see his ear poking out and it was pointed. I said, "You have pointed ears I knew it," and ran over to him and gave him a hug. I have always loved the faerie and so told him I love you, for allowing me to see him in my dream. He seemed to act like he did not know what to say, and I said, "But you do not want to hear that do you?" He then showed me a necklace he had on that was all white silver in the shape of two hands with the fingers touching to form a cage up to the wrists. Only there was nothing in it. I noticed this and felt like he was telling me that this is where his heart would go but now while he was separated from his heart, his feelings were gone as well to give him time to absorb all he had learned in life without the emotional weight of it so the necklace is what he wore until he decided to go try again. Then I woke up at home and remembered all of this and began looking up The Rad. I thought at first it was the faerie rad or ride when they change residence on August 7. I found out differently later though.

On August 14, 2006 I woke at 4:30 in the morning with another truth firmly planted in my mind. Some years earlier I had met Osiris for the first time in a lucid dream with my daughter along. During the experience he kept asking me as I met first Anubis, then him and then Set, if they were evil? Both the why of the question and why it was asked ofme I would ponder for some time. I decided after much thought it was to get my view of these beliefs and also of these beings. See I feel we all make mistakes and thus no one is really evil and to say they are, says that no one can learn and change or evolve. I said as much to Osiris at the time and I still believe it. I thought at the time it was a general question he asked everyone, but I was wrong.

This was just the beginning of a process of me remembering who and what I am. I, up until this point in my life, like I am sure many of you reading this, had studied many of the eastern religions, occult, meditation and all the new age dealings in an attempt to find the truth. It has only been since this happened to me that my beliefs have come almost but not quite full circle in that the angels took on much more meaning in my life. Not just the angels though, also the Sidhe or family as I refer to them. I knew that somehow I was here to help them also. To me there is no reason why the Sidhe and humanity should not be able to live together on the planet, in fact I feel humanity at this point in time would greatly benefit from it.

As I am writing this, I want you to know I am sitting here in a complete state of awe. This realization has changed my life profoundly and I believe will change this world we live in. While I have been communicating with them over the last eight years, I have been getting answers to questions I asked that sometimes took days, weeks, months and even years. The reason is comprehension. They want to make sure when we ask a question that we as an individual completely comprehend the answer, and depending on a persons blocks or openness, is how long it takes. They are moving in, through, and around these blocks so that I as an individual would fully comprehend their answers in the most clear way possible. They do this using telepathy, words, pictures and actual events within our lives. Yes they have actually affected my life on numerous occasions. Sometimes we will have to comprehend one part first, before we are able to fully comprehend the answer to our question, thus it can take some time. It was during this process I realized there is such a thing as gods and that they were alive and kicking so to speak.

They had not left us way back when, but simply faded into the background to give humanity a chance to make headway on their own. From time to time they have come into certain peoples lives and made themselves known to them, to help them at a point in their evolution where they needed to understand more. They have always been here. Just like the mother Earth, Gaia, Hera, Lilith, Nephthys, Babalon or what ever other name you want to call her, has always been here with us. Incarnating right along side us so that humanity would have a chance to evolve. Many times the persona and ego do not know that their soul and spirit are one of the masters. Instead what happens is they begin channeling information way above their own thought processes, and this is how the gods and goddesses have helped humanity evolve. By going through the same processes as all the other younger spirits and souls are going through at the same time. Learning does not stop once you achieve your goal. There is always more to learn. The gods learn from us, just like we learn from them.

Some time back I read an article where someone mentioned demons. It was during this time that I went and asked Osiris if there was such a thing. Wait... Stay open here... I asked this already knowing that a human is a spirit and a soul in a body. Knowing this, and also knowing angels were spirits, and that when we died our spirits were separated from our souls while in transition. I was having a hard time reconciling the very idea of "demons". In response to my question, he asked me, "What is the difference between a spirit and a demon?" If, I reasoned that a demon was a spirit without a soul, then why were the angels not demons also? Yet I could not even conceive of these beings as demons. The answers was because they had not lost their soul, because they never had one to loose. Only upon entering into life on earth did they receive a soul and a body, and unless they merge with that soul during their lifetime, then at the end they are separated from their soul to consider what they have learned thus far about souls and incarnate again if they choose to try again. So then I thought are these spirits who have died as humans then demons? That would make everyone who had died and had not become enlightened, a demon, and that made no sense either. So then breaking rules came up and I reasoned that those souls who had sinned would be demons and loose their souls. Then this was the cause of Karma and created the never ending cycle that so few found a way out of. The only problem with this, was how was a spirit to learn and teach his soul without making mistakes sometimes? So I could not even call those who had sinned demons, for they had a right to learn and evolve, and to say otherwise would in fact create Karma of my own by holding them back from learning in the way they needed to learn. Not everyone learns the same. For a good week now I have been pondering this and this morning, Osiris said to me, "De-man". That was all he had to say at this point for me, and hopefully if l have chosen my words correctly then many of you just got that also. There is truly no such thing as a demon in the way humans mean it, as in unearthly monsters that eat humans or feed on them or influence them towards negativity. There are no monsters, we are all spirits and souls learning. To kill someone while they are living simply means that when the separation occurs, for your spirit to consider what it has learned it will take it some time to reconcile what it allowed your ego to do. So whoever thought up Demon was simply prejudice and in fact seeing themselves as better because they were at that moment in a body and so suffering from the sin of pride or they were simply superstitious, and being very irresponsible for their own errors. To De-man means to separate the soul from the spirit which only happens when we die before merging our two halves, which happens to the majority of humans until they become enlightened and evolve. The body really has nothing to do with it, as it is a vehicle. De mans(a spirit who is without soul) only want love(the soul back as soul equals heart/love).

This morning I went out on my deck to water the plants and poured water on a tree frog hiding in one of 1:llY plants. He jumped out and I grabbed him before my dog or cats could. He sat on my hand and crawled around on me for a few minutes not afraid at all and I finally found a good place to put him that was safe. I went to the next town to see my mother and came back and the same Dove that had flew in front of me sometime back flew up into a tree right above me while I was locking the gate and sat there in full view and called to me. I spoke to it and asked it if it had been watching the place for me and it cooed and I thanked it and cooed back and it then flew up higher into another fir tree. I feel quite honored by this dove and his mate. He is also one of the biggest ring neck doves I have ever seen. I used to own a pair that had babies and I set them free. I can not help but wonder, except that was in another state. Still anything is possible.

It is simply amazing to me how the spirits and gods communicate with me. I will ask something and get an answer very indirectly, but I always get an answer. Since I had the dream about The Rad, I had thought I figured it out but it was still running through my mind. Then a few days ago (8/21/06) I was looking up the goddess Bat from Egyptian legends and found a reference to a half month called The Rad. It begins with the birthday of Hathor on August 29th. Bat was a cow eared goddess also and basically turned into Hathor as time went on. Did she reincarnate? I find this interesting that this half month has to do with the extension of the goddess I was researching weeks later, and that it is to take place in a week. Further I found out that it is also a rune. I have never read up on runes so was unaware of this association. The particular rune called Rad apparently has to do with union, re-union, travel, new jobs, rebirth of the soul, and it also means

Red. I have red hair. It also refers to change and a spiritual

journey or the path we take, and can also have to do with

the reunion of spirit and soul. In that sense it could also

mean contact, re-union of those that began our race. I

guess we will see and you will too as I am writing this. So

not only am I writing of all the magical experiences that I

have had in my life, but my friends the Sidhe, the faerie, the

grays, the Gods and Goddesses are all helping too. I found

four journals I have been looking for and added a few more

lines to this book so maybe this was "The Rad" they were

referring to. My continuing pathway and desire to bring

the magic of life back to Earth. I have been wondering what

to title it and The Rad does fit.

On the twelfth of September, I was taking pictures of

my yard. It was beginning to change so I try to capture the

changes on film. At one point I looked in the viewfinder

for my digital camera and saw something white in front

of my twenty foot Rhododendron. I pulled the camera

away from my eyes and still saw something white but

could not make out what it was. So I snapped a picture,

with the intention of blowing it up further to figure it out. There it was when I down loaded it all over the picture like I had seen it moving. Looking like a Frisbee. In the picture if I can manage to get it blown up for this book, there are a few men standing in the bottom left comer that look overlapped as if two dimensions are overlapped in the picture. I think that is what is happening in it. I had invited the Sidhe to visit any time they wanted to, and I know how they like gardens. There is one man who looks like he is overlapped on a branch and seems to be holding a remote control controller in his hands. The others appear to be watching the white objects fly around. This was still during the period of the Rad. A week or so later, six pileated woodpeckers showed up and began flying around my yard playing and chasing each other. They sound just like woody woodpecker the cartoon I watched as a kid. I look at anima als differently now after so many experiences with them. It is just as easy for a spirit to enter an animal as it is for a spirit to enter a human body. For that matter it is just as easy for a spirit, who are shape shifters to change into an animal, or anything else they please. After all they can learn quit a bit as animals, not just as being animals but from watching humans. Not that all animals are spirits but many could be. Last summer a robin flew into my double pane window in the front. I ran outside to see what had hit the window as I had been in the back and had only heard the sound. As I looked through the bushes a robin was sitting on the ground stunned. I looked at it and pet it and talked to it for a while. I put some water next to it and thought I would give it a few minutes to see if it would take off by itself. My cats wanted out and I did not want to let them out until I knew he was ok. About fifteen minutes later I came out and he was still there and seemed to be falling asleep. I pet him and sent him healing energy. I told him I wanted to make sure he could fly before I let my cats out. He looked at me and seemed to understand and flew across the yard. The next few days a robin was hanging around the house right off my deck when ever I went out, and where I could not be certain, I think it was him.

Out of superstition and fear, there has been too much kept from humanity. Human view points from centuries ago are accepted as gospel when comparatively those people were back in the dark ages from what we now

understand on an emotional level. People have been made

to feel afraid if they research anything to do with aliens

or faeries by humans afraid of loosing their own positions

of power. Anyone speaking about it in mixed crowds is

hushed up or ridiculed for fear of it coming back on their

career or some other part of their life. If you want proof of

this, start researching it for yourself and see what happens.

I can not tell you how many psychics have told me how

shocked they were when their friends or relatives began

telling them they were crazy when they made a discovery

and shared it with them. Or how a relationship began with

their boyfriend knowing all about their psychic talents

only to have them expect them to just drop their interests

completely when their guys' friends decided it was weird.

Considering how many have seen grays, reptiles and

ships of various sorts, I think it is high time the rest of the

human race wakes up to the fact that the earth is round.

After all most people are only afraid because they are

different and as soon as they learn about them that fear

goes away. Even those who have been researching these

subjects still have much to learn. Parsons for example, when he brought in the spirit of Babalon she called him a fool. Because she had already been incarnating along with us and even he did not realize it. Here he thought the world needed love, men needed love and he and Crowley thought this was what would save humanity from the looming disaster that they were heading for. Yet love has been here all along, only I guess she was not speaking loud enough. Humanity expects the gods to be perfect and the part of humanity that expects them to be perfect is the ego. Rather humorous when you realize the ego was created by the spirits in the first place. Spirits know everything because they are all connected. They are the mind, the same mind Carlos Castaneda spoke of when he said, "They gave us their mind." The ego runs the brain and is a receptor/ transmitter of the mind with a memory. It is not the mind, but because of its connection as a middleman it has begun to take advantage of its position. It is through those very memories that the ego will live on within the spirit. If the ego will accept its station and stand down so that the soul and spirit can merge, then the ego and persona will take on new form within an enlightened being. So what the ego fights and thinks of its own downfall and destruction, is really evolution into a new form. Just as your astral body contains persona and ego aspects, when your soul and spirit merge this astral body will then become your new body and live so long it will seem forever. When people begin to realize this and live with this knowledge then much of the fear passed around by the ego will vanish. Love is understanding.

The spirit knows everything and the soul understands everything. There is a very distinct difference. To know something you do not need to understand it. The soul, because it is able to understanding everything, it does not need to know it for it has an imagination to create anything. Imagination is not born of knowing, it is borne out of understanding and this is the gift of the soul. When a being that knows everything and a being that understands everything merge as one, well I think you can see the possibilities of gods. This will only occur if and when both parties accept each other as equal. Now most people I think have learned that as above-so below means as things are in heaven so they are on earth. This includes within earth and so as within -so without also applies in a very literal sense. Females are more in tune with souls, and males are more in tune with spirits, hence as within-so without. So any relationship problems you are having in your outside life is directly related to your issues going on between your soul and spirit. I say this because many on Earth have begun to think they can live without the opposite sex, or relationships, and what this points to is a spirit or soul giving up on the merging. Hopefully after a brief pause they try again, but both can leave and in each case it is not good for the body. Sometimes the spirit gives up and then there are other spirits who have been waiting for a chance and this is the cause of many walk-ins. Humanity or rather egos have been very freaked out by this, seeing this as possession because the spirit that created the ego is now different and taking possession of the ego. Something like having a new step-father in the home and the son having to learn to take a different sort of direction. However the only other alternative is to be a headless tube, mindless. It is much worse if the soul gives up, for then the body dies. I am hoping this will give food for thought to the egos in this world, so they may better see what their machinations are getting them.

Too much of this worlds societies are based on the egos apparent needs, instead of on the needs of soul and spirit to understand one another and learn to work with each other. Including more spirituality within societies curriculum will spur growth and will change the world for the better. Anything that pushes fear is of the egos, for that is what the ego uses to get the soul to focus on the negative and thus steal the souls imagination. Worry is one of the worst things you can do, for you are allowing your imagination to be stolen by the ego, to create what you are worrying about. Instead of worrying about anything, simply wrap yourself in white light from the bottom of your feet to the top of your head about three times. Three times should do it but in case you have a terribly stubborn ego you may continue doing this until it lets go of your imagination and then, "Imagine what you feel would be better than what you were worrying about." See this, visualize it and then know that it will be in some form that your spirit gives to you. Do not put limits on your spirit, if you limit your air it stagnates. Let the mind be free to create from what you have given it through your imagination. Focus only on the light. That means focus on what you want in your life not what you do not want. It does not mean that all is sugar and spice, it means others may screw up their relationships but you do not have to focus on this unless you want it in your life. You need to start asking yourself if you need to experience what you are experiencing? Or do you have your brain(ego) on automatic accepting in all thoughts whether you want them or not, like a kid in a candy store that can not make up his mind which candy he wants. Or falling asleep with a TV going so they can tell your spirit what you want in your life. Evolving means taking control of your imagination, feelings, and thoughts and becoming responsible for what you allow in your life. Own your imagination, own your thoughts, own your feelings and watch your life change for the better. To be aware of these things is the next step for humanity. There are many ways to take back your imagination. There are many manifestation teachers out there and each one I have listened to has taught me something different, a tool to use. If you have a partner, using, "Not for me," is a great beginning for they can help you catch yourself. Using this phrase every time you catch yourself focusing on anything you do not want in your life, will put the breaks on your thoughts going forward. Doing this will only allow those thoughts that you really want in your life to get created or manifested in your world. However those thoughts from previous days and times, will still run their course and their manifestation will even speed up because you are no longer allowing negative thoughts in. If you continue for a couple weeks with this, you should find that many of the things you want in your life have begun to manifest and in some cases almost immediately, depending on your feelings, intentions and how much focus you put out on it. Now I mentioned if you have a partner in the beginning and I want to point out that having someone to do this with helps immensely because they can help you catch yourself. Sometimes we want something in our life but every time we focus on it, other thoughts come in to our mind that counteracts our desire. This is your ego(brain) trying to regain control and it is so subtle, and you may be so used to it that it just flies right past you without your awareness of the thought. This is where your friend or partner can help you catch yourself. It also helps if you can see your ego with compassion and understanding of its fear of loosing control. After all it is the brain. The brain was never meant to control the soul, but because it was created by the mind(spirit), it translates in an intellectual manner what it receives from the soul. This is fine until such time as the soul wakes up and learns to think with its heart. I believe this is one area where the idea of demons and spirits being evil came from. Thoughts coming into the brain from your soul or spirit made the ego aware that it was not alone. It is not god, and more importantly was not in complete control. The ego saw this as leading to chaos, and directly against it's will to survive that was programmed in to give the best chance to the soul for survival when the body is still in its infancy. So the soul trying to wake up and spirit trying to help the soul, were portrayed as the bad guys. Demons trying to possess you. This is also a reason why much of the occult knowledge has been kept secret for so long To protect those awakening from the egos of people not ready to deal with the truth. Only it has been twisted somewhat I feel for I have found that if a person is ready to receive information they will in some capacity even if they do not at first accept it. If they are not ready then they will not understand it at all, and not even try to. People do not go mad because of information or faint like some Southern belle from when they wore corsets. They may begin to realize how a select group of people control them by convincing them they are weak and really do not want to deal with this stuff. Let others more accomplished do it, they know what they are doing. Meaning you do not. Because they are insecure with this subject they do not pursue the matter further. Anyone trying to get to the answers within their family or friends is then told they are crazy, troublemakers, or worse possessed so they can save face in front of their social group and not look like they do not know everything. This is the ego, otherwise known as the Borg that does not know everything and only receives from the spirit and pulls from prior memory. You may ask why if the spirit created the ego does it not stop this behavior. The answer is two fold. First the spirit is not inside the body and has not been since Osiris was slaughtered. Only occasionally do the spirits come into body, like when someone becomes enlightened or just prior to it. The other answer is that the spirit itself is trying to get the soul to stand up for itself and control the ego itself. When this happens the spirit is able to respect and see the soul as an equal. Remember we are two different beings. We have the mind of the spirit who is the greater mind, and sees things from a very intellectual stance. Then we have the instinct of the soul who is emotional. To the spirit, if the soul can not stand her ground with the ego then how is she equal to the spirit. Remember to the spirit love means anything the soul admires, allows in her space or pays attention to. This is a very intellectual view of love.

The soul offers the spirit something that it does not normally experience and that is feelings and understanding. The soul feels things as in intuition and empathy. This makes the soul much better able to read the spirit than the spirit is able to read the soul. To the spirit, emotions are chaotic and they have a hard time trusting them, especially when the soul makes decisions based on feelings rather than on logic. These are decisions the spirit does not "know." The soul has the ability to feel if something is right based on the understanding of empathy. The soul does not like to make decisions where it does not inherently feel the rightness because to it, there is something not right. It may not know what this something is, but it feels and understands that it is not right. So in order for humanity to progress the soul has to take control of it's life. It has to come off automatic and control it's thoughts by only allowing thoughts in it's brain that it wants in it's life. The soul, by using it's imagination to create light, and not allowing the ego to focus on darkness, puts the ego in a better controlled environment so it will not be *as* fearful of chaos. It will gain new respect for the soul and accept the souls right to control. The soul for it's part, by proving to the spirit that it could handle itself with the ego, will not only have gained the admiration of the spirit but the self confidence to stand up for its equality with the spirit.

Remember to the spirit admiration is love and this will open the door to many more humans becoming merged in the hermetic marriage, or in other words becoming enlightened. When you understand this, then you will be on you way to merging into the godhead and making beautiful music together.